STRIP
QUILTING

Merry Christmas, Nancy
1991

Love, Jeannie

STRIP QUILTING

Diane Wold

TAB BOOKS
Blue Ridge Summit, PA

FIRST EDITION
FIFTH PRINTING

© 1987 by **Diane Wold**.
Published by TAB BOOKS.
TAB BOOKS is a division of McGraw-Hill, Inc.

Library of Congress Cataloging-in-Publication Data

Wold, Diane.
   Strip quilting.
   Includes index.
   1. Quilting.   I. Title.
TT835.W64   1987   746.9′7   87-10008
ISBN 0-8306-2522-4
ISBN 0-8306-2822-3 (pbk.)

TAB BOOKS offers software for sale. For information and a catalog, please contact TAB Software Department, Blue Ridge Summit, PA 17294-0850.

Questions regarding the content of this book should be addressed to:

Reader Inquiry Branch
TAB BOOKS
Blue Ridge Summit, PA 17294-0850

Edited by Suzanne L. Cheatle
Designed by Jaclyn J. Boone

Contents

Introduction   **vii**

1 An Overview   **1**
Ancesters and Relatives — Design Principles — Designs

2 Tools and Techniques   **11**
Cutting Stripping — Marking Cross-Cut Lines — Sewing Strips Together —
Cutting and Sewing Segments

3 Instructions for a Come-On Quilt   **23**
Arranging Fabrics within the Pattern — Planning the Strips — Constructing the Quilt —
Come-On Place Mats

4 Turning a Quilt Top into a Quilt   **43**
Borders — Backing — Batting — Marking the Quilting Pattern — Basting — Quilting —
Binding — Signing the Quilt

5 Multiple-Band Patterns   **61**
Two-Band Patterns — Patterns Using Three Bands — Patterns from Four or More Bands

6 Choosing Fabrics and Colors   **89**
Color — Pattern — Combining Fabrics: Your Personal Style

7 One-Band Shift Patterns   **97**
The Loop-and-Shift Technique — Creating Curves by Varying Segment Widths —
Creating Curves by Varying Offsets — Other Variations

8 Shifted Multiple-Band Patterns   **121**
Plus Signs — Ziggurats — Half-Drop Patterns — Hungarian Point

9 Designing Your Own Quilts   **159**
Resizing — Preparing a Table for a New Pattern — Figuring Yardage — Adapting
Designs — Methods for Original Design

Index   **174**

Introduction

Strip piecing or *piecing and repiecing* is a fast way to construct quilt tops on a sewing machine. Because a typical pieced and repieced quilt is composed of hundreds of rectangular pieces, it doesn't look easy to make. Indeed, if it were pieced using traditional methods, the first step would be to cut out all those little rectangles—a long and tedious task. If the pattern is pieced and repieced, however, then only long, straight cuts, and long, straight seams are made, and the process is, in fact, fast and easy.

This book contains complete instructions, including diagrams, cutting instructions, and a shopping list, for each of the projects illustrated. Pointers are given for modifying projects in this book, for adapting patterns from other sources, and for creating your own designs.

The designs in this book follow the paths I have taken in making strip-pieced quilts. First I made a quilt that used a Seminole patchwork pattern on a large scale. Then I realized that I could make a new pattern, Come-On, using the Seminole patchwork technique. Later, I figured out how to make patterns inspired by bargello needlepoint and other needlework sources.

I've started experimenting with some additional methods, while others are still only fuzzy ideas in the back of my head. I also keep returning to my first methods and finding new and exciting patterns there. The same old patterns still yield new possibilities. I've made half a dozen Come-On quilts, and enjoyed each one.

Your Come-On quilt, or any other quilt you make following instructions in this book, will be unique because you will have selected the fabrics of which it is made. You might modify a pattern given here, thereby creating your own pattern. You might find a needlepoint pattern or a weaving pattern that you can adapt to piecing and repiecing. As I discovered how to "loop and shift," you might discover a new design principle that will make it possible to piece new types of patterns.

The practical advantages of piecing and repiecing remain the same: ease, speed, and economy of construction. The creative enjoyment you have in making a pieced and repieced quilt will include choosing the fabrics and the pattern, and might extend to discovering profound innovations in technique.

Chapter 1
An
Overview

Figures 1–1 through 1–4 show the steps involved in constructing a typical pieced and repieced quilt, and introduce the terminology used in this book. First, long *strips* of fabric are sewn together into striped *bands*. These bands then are cut up into *segments,* and the segments are sewn together to make the *pattern.* The pattern is composed of rectangles, but the rectangles have been cut in two stages. The first stage was the cutting of the strips, and the second was the cutting of the segments. At both stages, long, thin strips, rather than little rectangles, have been cut.

The straight cuts all can be marked and cut with a ruler, a pencil, and a good pair of sewing shears. The work can go faster, however, with some special tools. Marking can be speeded up with a clear plastic ruler designed for strip quilting. Cutting can be faster with a rotary cutter and a special cutting pad. These tools, and the techniques for using them, are described in Chapter 2, *Tools and Techniques.*

For pieced and repieced quilts, all the sewing, like the cutting, is long and straight. All seams are sewn on a sewing machine. In fact, this technique won't work by hand. When the bands are cut into segments, the stitching that holds the strips together is cut. A sewing machine uses a lockstitch, which won't unravel when cut this way, but a hand running stitch would. Pieced and repieced quilts must be made on a sewing machine, but any sewing machine will work, since all that's required is a straight stitch. If you plan to use a sewing machine for the *quilting* (the stitching that holds together top, batting, and back), then you might find a special foot or attachment useful. Sewing machines and attachments also are described in Chapter 2.

The pattern shown in Fig. 1–4 was adapted from an inkle weaving pattern called Come-On. Chapter 3, *Instructions for a Come-On Quilt,* contains directions for making this pattern as a crib-sized quilt in four different color schemes. Beginners probably will want to start by making a Come-On quilt, since the instructions for this quilt are given in greater detail than for the others in this book. Experienced quilters might read this chapter and immediately apply the methods to another pattern.

Piecing and repiecing produces a pieced fabric, which might be intended for a quilt, place mats, clothing, or other purposes, but which is usually quilted. Chapter 4, *Turning a Quilt Top into a Quilt,* contains information on borders, backings, and battings, as well as instructions for basting, quilting, and binding a quilt.

Strips for Band A   Strips for Band B

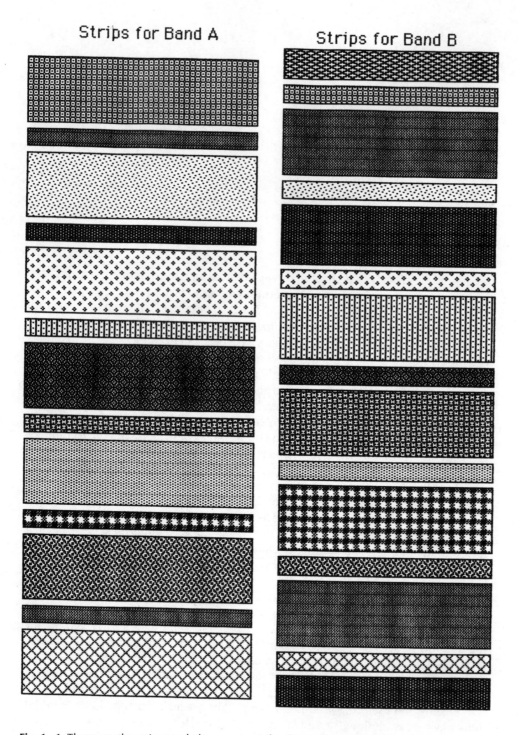

Fig. 1–1. These are the *strips* needed to construct the Come-On pattern.

Band A   Band B

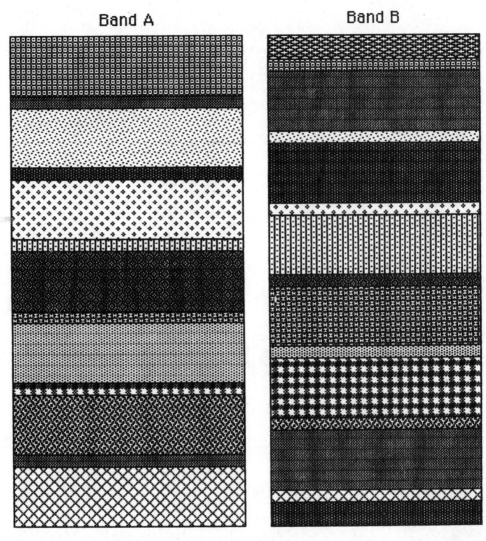

Fig. 1–2. The strips have been sewn together to form the two *bands* needed for the Come-On pattern.

Segments

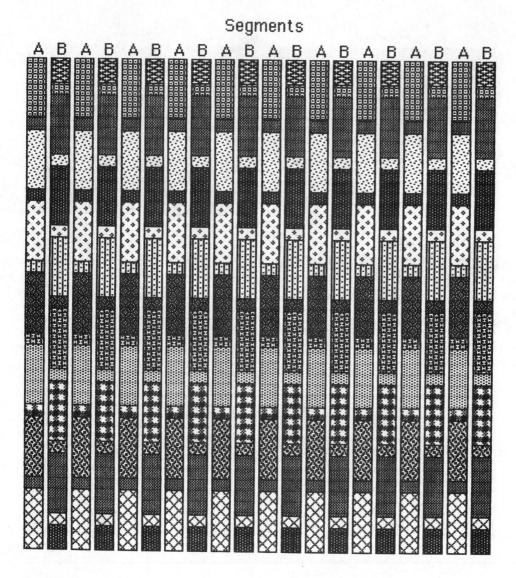

Fig. 1–3. The vertical *segments* are labeled A and B to show from which band they were cut.

Pattern

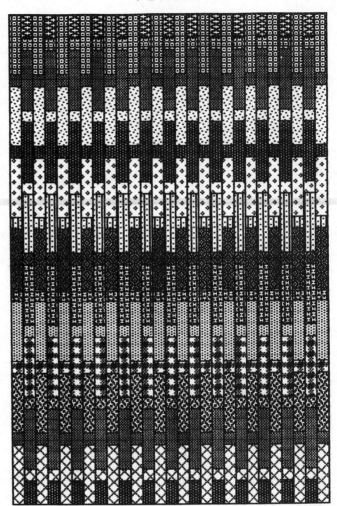

Fig. 1–4. The segments have been sewn together to form the Come-On *pattern area.*

ANCESTORS AND RELATIVES

The piecing and repiecing technique is based on Seminole patchwork, which is typically constructed as in Fig. 1 – 5. In the example, three patterns are sewn together with several plain strips of fabric. This kind of patchwork was invented by the Seminole Indians of Florida. It is one of those instant folk arts that sprang up when manufactured cloth was introduced to a "primitive" culture. In the case of the Seminoles, manufactured cloth and sewing machines both were introduced in the late nineteenth century. The distinctive Seminole patchwork is made by tearing strips of cloth, sewing them together into bands, cutting up the bands into segments, and then arranging different segments to make a pattern. In other words, the basic piecing and repiecing technique is exactly the same as the Seminole patchwork technique.

The most obvious differences between Seminole patchwork and pieced and repieced quilts are scale and proportion. Seminole patchwork is used to produce narrow patterned strips of fabric, which are used like decorative braid in the construction of clothing. It is typically composed of pieces that are ¼ inch to 1 inch square, while the rectangles in a pieced and repieced quilt are typically 1 inch wide and 2 to 6 inches long. Seminole patchwork produces a long, narrow piece, with one *row* of pattern. A pieced and repieced quilt is more nearly square, and usually appears to contain several rows of pattern.

Other quilting methods have been inspired by Seminole patchwork, and the whole group of methods is known as *strip piecing,* or *strip quilting.* Strip piecing covers a wide variety of techniques, which can be used to produce a wide variety of results. Some strip-piecing methods are shortcuts for producing traditional quilt patterns. Some quiltmakers use strip-piecing techniques to produce striped or specially patterned fabric, which they then incorporate into their work. Piecing and repiecing produces patterned fabrics, which are used directly as quilt tops and look different from traditional quilts.

DESIGN PRINCIPLES

The different "look" of piecing and repiecing results largely from two principles I follow in designing these quilts. The first principle is meant to make sewing easier; the second, to avoid wasted cloth.

I make sewing easier by planning the seams between segments so that the rectangles meet in easy T-joins rather than in more difficult X-joins. The trouble with X-joins is that they must be pinned before sewing and must be matched exactly to look really good. If two segments meet in T-joins, then the seam between them can slip slightly without any obvious mismatching. The top pattern in Fig. 1 – 5 shows a Seminole patchwork pattern full of X-joins, while the second contains only T-joins.

I also plan patterns to minimize wasted fabric. The third pattern in Fig. 1 – 5 shows a Seminole patchwork pattern that is composed of diamonds, or squares set diagonally. Each triangle on the edge of the pattern started as a square, but the excess was trimmed off. If this kind of construction were used on the scale of a quilt, the trimmings would be dozens of moderately large fabric triangles. I can't stand the idea of wasting this much fabric, or of using up all those little triangles in another project, so I don't use this kind of construction technique in pieced and repieced quilts.

6

Fig. 1–5. In this sample of Seminole patchwork, three patchwork strips, each of which would be constructed separately, have been sewn together with plain strips.

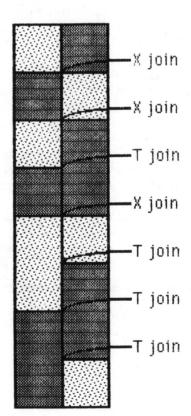

Fig. 1–6. This detail of the seam between two segments shows how pieces from the segments can come together in X-joins, which require careful matching, and T-joins, which do not.

As a result of using these two principles, I usually design patterns that are composed of rectangles, the kind of patterns that can be laid out on graph paper. There are many sources for such designs, including many other fiber arts, such as weaving, needlepoint, knitting, and counted cross-stitch. All of these needle arts are based on a square grid, and all can inspire pieced and repieced quilt designs.

DESIGNS

Our first pieced and repieced design, Come-On, is composed of two types of segments, which you will sew together alternately. Other designs based on this idea are contained in Chapter 5, *Multiple-Band Patterns*. The patterns in this chapter are composed of two, three, or more types of segments sewn together in regularly repeating patterns.

The fabrics and colors used in any pieced pattern are often as important as the piecing pattern itself. Chapter 6 discusses color theory briefly, using the quilts shown in the color plates as examples. Some practical techniques for building a color scheme are also discussed.

Chapter 7, *Single-Band Shift Patterns,* introduces a new piecing technique. Figure 1–7 shows how identical segments can be "shifted" up or down to produce a pattern. The pattern, as shown, has uneven edges, and simply trimming them off would violate my "no-waste" principle. Figures 1–8 and 1–9 show how the pattern can be cut across, and the two pieces of pattern rearranged to make a rectangle. The rectangles used to make the pattern area with the uneven edges shown in Fig. 1–7 are exactly the same rectangles needed to make the rectangular pattern area with the even edges in Fig. 1–9.

These diagrams do not, however, illustrate the way in which the pattern is actually sewn. Instead of the segments being sewn together, then the result cut apart and the pieces sewn together with a zigzag seam, each segment is made into a loop by sewing its ends together, and each loop is cut in the appropriate place before any segments are sewn together. This process is explained in detail in Chapter 7.

The patterns in Chapter 7 are all made by shifting segments of one type, but it is possible to use the looping-and-shifting technique in patterns composed of more than one segment type. These designs are explored in Chapter 8, *Multiple-Band Shift Patterns.*

What if you want to do something a little different? Chapter 9 shows how to do all the bookkeeping needed to calculate the strips and the yardage you'll need. Pointers are given for modifying projects in this book, for adapting patterns from other sources, and for creating your own designs.

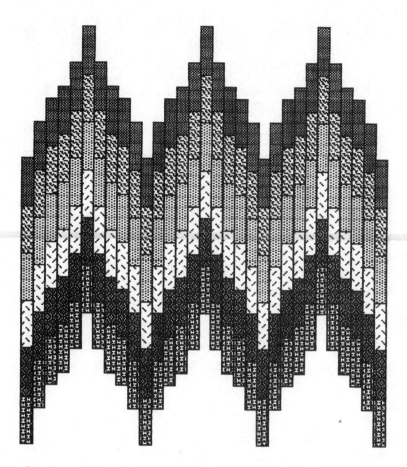

Fig. 1–7. Designs like this use segments from only one band. The segments are shifted up and down to create the pattern.

Fig. 1–8. The shifted pattern shown in Fig. 1–7 has been cut across horizontally, and the top piece has been moved under the bottom piece. Note how the zigzag edges of the two pieces fit together.

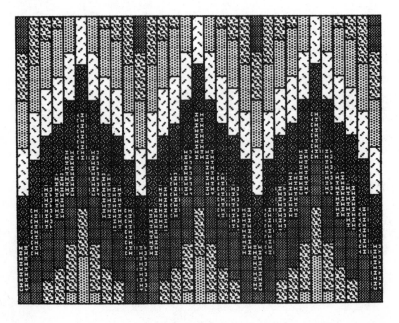

Fig. 1–9. The two pieces in Fig. 1–8 have been joined together to create a rectangular pattern area. The steps shown are not those used to sew a rectangular pattern area, but they show how segments from one band can be cut up and arranged to form such a pattern area.

Chapter 2
Tools and Techniques

Tools needed for making pieced and repieced quilts fall into three categories: general sewing tools; paper and measuring tools for planning, drafting, and marking; and the sewing machine and its attachments. A pieced and repieced quilt can be made with minimal tools of each type. Sewing tools you'll need are pins, needles, and sewing scissors. For planning and measuring, you'll need paper, a pencil, a ruler, and a large piece of corrugated cardboard. Any sewing machine will do.

Of course, there are other tools that you might want to use, or that you might buy as you become more involved in strip piecing. Some of these extra tools, though not necessary, do make the work easier. Some might speed things up so much that, once you own them, you'll feel you couldn't do without them.

The ideas behind piecing and repiecing were outlined in the last chapter. This chapter gives the nitty-gritty details of the measuring, cutting, and sewing. As I discuss each stage of the construction, I also will discuss the tools that are optional or necessary for that stage. Chapter 4 covers the process of turning this quilt top into a quilt.

CUTTING STRIPPING

Strips are only rectangles, but you must be sure that the strips you cut are even in width. Strips that have wavering edges or that are wider at one end than the other can lead to bands that won't lie flat or to segments that have differing lengths. These, in turn, can lead to patterns in which the pieces do not fit together as planned or which do not lie flat or are not square.

I usually cut strips that run across the grain of the fabric, from selvage to selvage. One reason I use this method is that I can get a long strip (the whole width of the fabric) out of even a remnant. Also, the stripes in striped fabric usually end up going the right way if I cut the strips across the grain. Finally, strips cut on the crosswise grain have a little more *give,* or stretch, than strips cut parallel to the selvage. This give makes it easier to sew strips together so that their lengths match up properly. Sometimes, when I'm using scrap fabric or with some fabric patterns, I will cut strips on the lengthwise grain.

Rather than marking and cutting each strip individually, I usually cut a quantity of *stripping,* fabric cut to the right width, but not yet cut to the right length. For some projects, I reserve part of the material for borders, and cut stripping across the remaining width, as shown in Fig. 2–1, but I usually cut stripping that runs all the way across the fabric and later cut the stripping into strips of the proper lengths. Cutting stripping across the whole width of the fabric might lead to leftover stripping, but the cutting process goes much faster.

Sometimes a pattern requires a strip that is longer than the width of the fabric, or than the scrap fabric you are using. In these cases, you can put together a strip out of shorter pieces of stripping. This step is accomplished while you are marking the cross-cut lines, as described in the next section.

The first step in cutting stripping from a length of fabric is to square off the end of the fabric, which is almost never square as purchased. Even when fabric has been torn from the bolt and is square, you still must trim the end, since tearing fabric distorts the torn edge. Once you have trimmed the end, you make stripping by cutting parallel to the trimmed end.

You can square the end by pulling a thread and cutting along it, by marking a line across the end and cutting along the line, or by squaring up a guide and cutting along the guide with a rotary cutter. Most of us have had a snag in a knit garment and are familiar with the look of a pulled thread in that context. Pulling a thread to cut by is simply creating such a snag on purpose and using the puckered line as a cutting guide. This method requires some skill, but only a pair of shears to cut with.

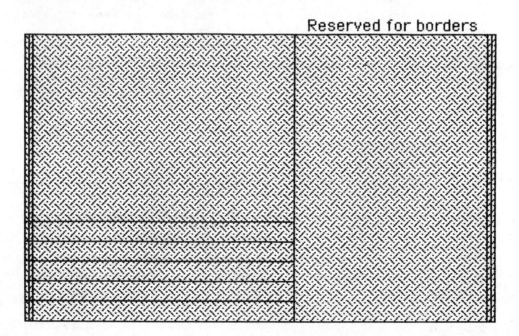

Fig. 2–1. Sometimes you might want to cut the fabric into two pieces along the lengthwise grain before you cut strips. One of the two pieces shown here will be used for the borders of the quilt, while the other will be used for strips.

Sewing Shears

Sewing shears are scissors—big ones designed to allow you to cut with long strokes. The main things to look for in shears are a comfortable, smooth action and sharpness. Sewing scissors will, of course, become dull with use, and need to be sharpened. Learn to sharpen your shears or find a cutlery shop or sewing store that provides a sharpening service, and use it. Like any other edged tools, scissors only work really well when they are sharp.

Triangles, Rulers, and Cutting Guides

If you decide to mark a line to cut by, you'll need a long ruler or some other straightedge, and a tool for squaring up your straightedge. A drafting triangle is the easiest right-angle tool to use, and is also useful for marking 45-degree lines, such as those needed for mitering corners. Triangles come in various sizes and qualities, and are available in dime stores or large drugstores, as well as in art or drafting supply stores. You don't need a fancy triangle, but bigger is better, since a bigger triangle makes it easier to mark an accurate right angle. The cardboard back of a tablet of paper can substitute for a triangle, since it has fairly square corners.

In theory, a straightedge can be any long piece of wood or metal with a straight edge, but in practice most edges are not as straight as they seem, and you'll probably want to use a ruler or a cutting guide. Most people own a yardstick, but this may not be a satisfactory tool, since it is longer than needed and since many yardsticks are cheaply made and might not have smooth, straight edges. Cutting guides are tools for marking parallel lines. Some are simple rectangles, designed for marking strips of just one width. They might come in a set containing guides of various widths. Some are rulers, usually of heavy, clear plastic, that have width markings as well as length markings.

Regular rulers also can be used and come in 18- and 24-inch lengths. The latter is preferable because it will reach across 45-inch fabric that has been folded in half. Some metal rulers have nonskid rubber backings, and some metal cutting guides have a sandpaperlike textured backing. You can keep any ruler from slipping by gluing small pieces of sandpaper to its back.

Marking Tools

A pencil is the usual tool for marking cutting lines. Sometimes, however, pencil doesn't show up on a particular fabric, so you must use some other marking tool. Do not use a ballpoint pen or felt marker. When the quilt is washed, the ink or dye might run onto the surface of the quilt and then become obstinately permanent.

I'm also wary of the blue "disappearing" felt-tip pens available in sewing stores. These pens make a blue line that fades when dampened. I've seen some disasters in which the "ink" reappeared as a brown line that seemed to be indelible. If you do use one of these pens, soak the work thoroughly to get the "ink" out of the fabric. Be very careful about ironing the work, since that seems to be one of the things that can set brown lines.

One old standby for marking dark fabrics is the cheapest: an old sliver of hand soap. The edge will make a reasonably thin white line, which shows up beautifully on dark fabrics. The soap will rub off with handling, but the mark should last long enough for most of our purposes. Other possibilities for marking dark fabric are chalk, dressmaker's chalk, white-colored pencils, soapstone pencils, and other special white markers you'll find in quilt specialty shops.

Fabrics that are not completely dark, but that have a very busy pattern, can be the hardest of all to mark. I've been most successful with a colored pencil in metallic silver. It makes a somewhat broader line than I would like, but its metallic sheen shows up well on almost all fabrics.

Marking Stripping

Fold the fabric by placing the selvages together. If the fabric is especially wide or your ruler is short, fold the fabric twice. Place the ruler or cutting guide across the end of the fabric, and keep it square with a drafting triangle or an improvised substitute. Mark a line for trimming the end of the fabric, then mark the lines for all the stripping you plan to cut. Pin the folded fabric to keep the layers from slipping while you're cutting. You'll also get less slipping if you cut with the fabric still on the table rather than picking it up in your hands.

Using a Rotary Cutter

A rotary cutter is like a pizza cutter, but smaller and much sharper. The cutter itself is not very expensive, but the special self-healing plastic cutting mat on which you cut is a more costly item. For cutting strips, you need a straightedge like one of those described previously. The cutting guides are natural companions to the rotary cutter; together they cut stripping very fast indeed.

Figure 2–2 shows how to even the edge of the fabric with a rotary cutter and a cutting guide. Put the cutter down at the far end of the fabric, with the blade resting against the edge of the straightedge, then pull the cutter toward you. Keep it snug to the ruler, and don't push down too hard. After you have trimmed the end of the fabric, turn the fabric 180 degrees, and make additional cuts, as shown in Fig. 2–3

The rotary cutter works so well because it's so sharp. It has a plastic guard, which you should push into place when you're not using the cutter. The only time I cut myself, I was doing two things wrong at once. I was using a dull blade, and I was cutting at an awkward angle. So, when your blade starts to dull, throw it away! Also, take the time to turn your fabric so that you're not cutting with your arms crossed or twisted, and so that you're cutting in a reasonable direction.

MARKING CROSS-CUT LINES

The cross-cut lines, shown as vertical lines in Fig. 2–4, are the lines along which you eventually will cut the bands into segments. The best time to mark these lines is after the strips are cut, but before they are sewn together into bands. When I first started, I marked the cross-cut lines when the bands were already sewn together, but I found that it was difficult to mark across seam allowances. It also can be hard to find a work surface large enough on which to spread out the band.

Marking the cross-cut lines, you also automatically measure and mark the length of the strips, and trim them to this length. I discovered the need to cut the strips to their proper length on my first pieced and repieced quilt, where I had merely cut pieces of stripping and sewn them together. I discovered, after I had cut most of the segments, that my machine fed the bottom layer of fabric a little more quickly than the top layer. In effect, one edge of each strip was stretched, leading to segments that were severely off grain. Since the fabrics I used were of slightly different widths, the pieces of stripping were of different lengths and I didn't notice the grain problem until I found myself cutting off-grain segments.

Making a Paper Template

The positions of the cross-cut lines depend on the pattern you are making. When I first started making pieced and repieced quilts, I individually measured all the positions of all the cross-cut lines on all the strips. Eventually I realized that I could do the measuring once, marking the positions of the cross-cut lines on a piece of paper, and then use the paper as a special ruler, marking all the strips from that.

Your paper template must be wider than the strips you'll be cutting, and at least as long. Since most strips are 2 to 6 inches wide, the width is not usually a problem. Finding a piece of paper 20 to 50 inches long might be harder, though. I use discarded computer paper, which comes accordian-folded in almost endless sheets. Most places with computers throw away reams of paper every week, and are glad to give some away. If you can't get discarded computer paper, you can buy shelf paper, or any other paper that comes in rolls.

Starting at one end, mark the positions of the cross-cut lines along one long edge of the paper. Do the same thing along the other edge of the paper and connect your marks. All the lines should be straight up and down; crooked lines mean you've made a mistake in measuring.

Using the Paper Template

When you mark your strips using the paper template, you'll place the template on a piece of corrugated cardboard, then lay the stripping on top of the paper template, and pin the stripping to the ruler by sticking pins all the way through into the piece of cardboard. I used to use a large piece of cardboard cut from the side of a box until that got lost, but now I use a cardboard cutting board of the type designed for cutting out clothing. It's marked in 1-inch squares, and folds up to about 1 × 3 feet for storage. In its folded form, my cutting board is sturdy and portable; I can lay it across my lap and mark strips while I'm watching television.

Before you start marking a piece of stripping, check the end and, if it's a selvage or is uneven, trim it. Lay the stripping, right side down, on top of the paper template. Line up the end of the stripping with the end of the paper ruler at which the measuring lines start. Stick pins through the corners of the stripping into the paper and the cardboard. Straighten out the stripping, being careful not to pull too tight, and pin the other end. Pinning the stripping in place usually makes it smooth and flat enough to mark on; however, if the strip is badly wrinkled, stop and press it before marking.

Fig. 2 – 2. The ruler and rotary cutter are in place for trimming the end of a piece of fabric. This particular cutting guide is wide enough so its corner can be used to square the edge. Thus no triangle is needed.

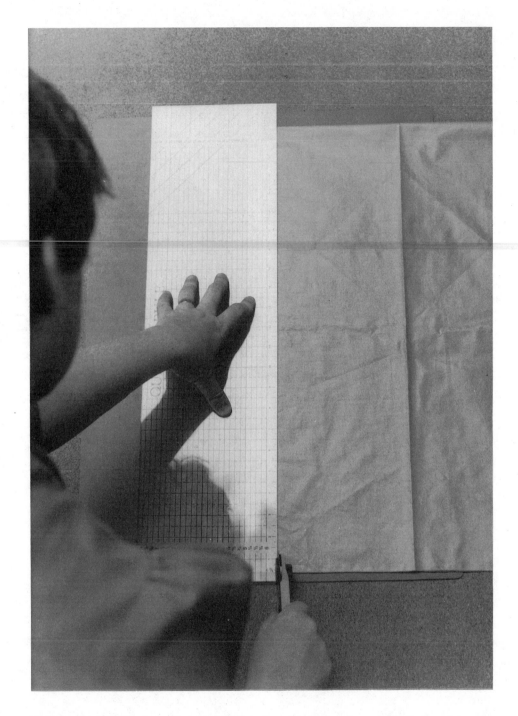

Fig. 2–3. The fabric has been turned 180 degrees from the position shown in Fig. 2–7., and the ruler and rotary cutter are in place for cutting a strip.

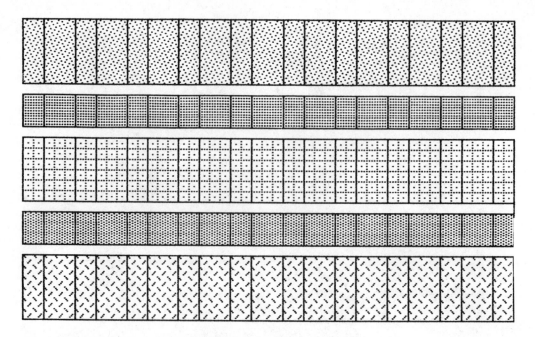

Fig. 2–4. The vertical lines shown here are the cross-cut lines. Once the strips have been sewn together into bands, the bands will be cut into segments along these lines.

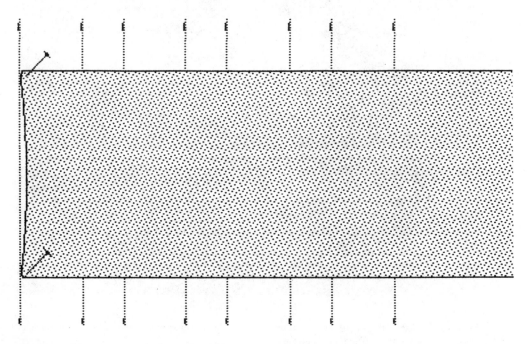

Fig. 2–5. A fabric strip is pinned onto the paper template. The end of the fabric scoops in slightly between the pins.

As shown in Fig. 2–5, the ends of the stripping will tend to scallop between the pins. If the scallop is very deep, you've probably pulled the stripping too tight. On wide stripping, a slight scoop is inevitable. You might want to put extra pins in the ends.

With the stripping in place, put a ruler across the stripping, and line it up with the first cross-cut line. Press down firmly on the ruler, since it holds the stripping in place, as well as acts as a marking guide. Draw along the edge of the ruler, as shown in Fig. 2–6. Continue until you've marked all the cross-cut lines. Unpin the stripping and trim the excess stripping along the last line.

Any ruler can be used for marking cross-cut lines, but I do have a favorite: the Dritz Vue-Thru Dressmakers Gauge. It's wide, so it holds the strip down securely; it's clear plastic, so it is easier for me to see what I'm doing; and it's only 6 inches long, so I don't need to worry about maneuvering extra length. The extra width is the biggest advantage, something that's otherwise hard to find except in an extra-long ruler.

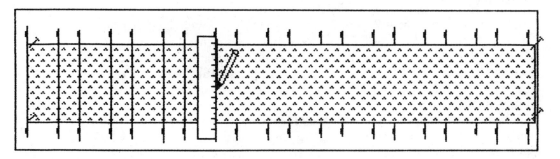

Fig. 2–6. A ruler is lined up with the vertical lines on the paper template and used to draw the cross-cut line on the fabric.

Piecing within Strips

Sometimes it is necessary to use two short pieces of stripping to make up one strip. Eventually you will cut the strip at each cross-cut line, so piecing the stripping at one of these lines simply anticipates a cut.

Start the first piece of stripping as usual, and mark as many cross-cut lines as possible. Trim the stripping at the last line you were able to mark, then pin it back in place on the paper template. Take another piece of stripping and pin it to the paper template, starting where the first piece of stripping left off, as shown in Fig. 2–7. Mark the remaining cross-cut lines, and trim the end as usual. You can, of course, use three or more pieces of stripping to construct a strip if necessary.

SEWING STRIPS TOGETHER

Sewing strips together into a band is one of the fastest steps in making a pieced and repieced quilt. The only tools required are pins, a sewing machine, and a guide for sewing even quarter-inch seams.

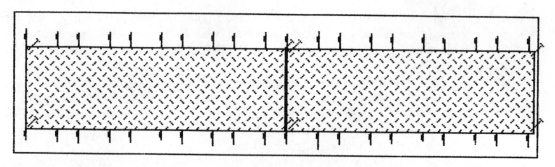

Fig. 2–7. A piece of stripping shorter than the desired strip was placed on the left-hand end of the paper template. It was trimmed at one of the cross-cut lines and pinned. Another piece of stripping was pinned to the template, starting where the first piece ended.

The Sewing Machine

Any sewing machine will work for making pieced and repieced quilts because only straight stitching is needed. If you don't do much sewing, this kind of straight stitching is a good opportunity to make friends with your machine and learn how to clean and oil it. Periodically, I realize that my machine is getting noisy, and so I open it up, remove the bobbin, brush dust out from around the bobbin case, and then drop oil into all the oil holes.

Quarter-inch seams are specified in all the instructions in this book. I find that ¼ inch is wide enough for almost all situations as long as the seam is even in width. A quarter-inch seam allowance that wavered from ⅛ inch to ⅜ inch in width could pull out in the narrow spots. A wavering seam, even a wide one, also leads to bands that don't lie flat. If you use fabrics that are especially prone to raveling, they might require special reinforcement of the seam allowances, but this is not necessary for the types of fabric usually used in quilt making.

To sew a quarter-inch seam, you need a guide of some sort. Many sewing machines have guidelines for various widths of seams marked on the faceplate, the metal plate under the presser foot. Unfortunately, these guidelines often do not include one for a quarter-inch seam. If your faceplate does not have a ¼ inch guideline, you still might be able to improvise one by putting a piece of tape on the faceplate. You might find, especially on a zigzag machine, that a piece of tape placed ¼ inch from the needle will cover part of the hole for the feed dog, and thus be unsatisfactory.

Another way to gauge a seam allowance is to line up the edges of the fabric with some feature on the presser foot. If you decide to use a presser foot to gauge your quarter-inch seams, you'll need to find a gauging mark by trial and error. This is a popular method, however, so it works with many machines and many presser feet.

Matching and Pinning

Before you sew the strips, place them together, matching the cross-cut lines. You have cut the strips to the same length, so their ends should match. Pin the strips as often as you like: I often pin only every foot or so, but you can pin at every cross-cut line if you prefer. If you've had to piece together any of your strips, the ends of the short pieces of stripping should be pinned.

CUTTING AND SEWING SEGMENTS

After you have sewn the strips together into a band, turn the band over and look at the cross-cut lines on the back. They should join up end to end to make one long cutting line. Little discrepancies ⅛ inch or less can be dealt with, but if any of the lines are badly mismatched, rip out the appropriate seams and resew them.

Start at one end of the first cross-cut line and cut along it. Cutting exactly on the marked line is not as important as cutting smoothly. If the cut line wobbles badly, the quarter-inch seams with which you'll be sewing the segments together might actually be much narrower in places, and fraying of the seam allowance could weaken the seam so that it comes apart. Pressing the band might make smooth cutting easier. If the cutting lines in two segments do not quite match up, cut between them, as shown in Fig. 2–8.

The natural impulse is to cut all the segments before you start to sew, but it is better to cut each segment just before you will sew it into place. If you cut all of the segments at once, handling them later might cause the fabric to fray and the stitching that has been cut to unravel. Cutting the segments as you need them also makes it

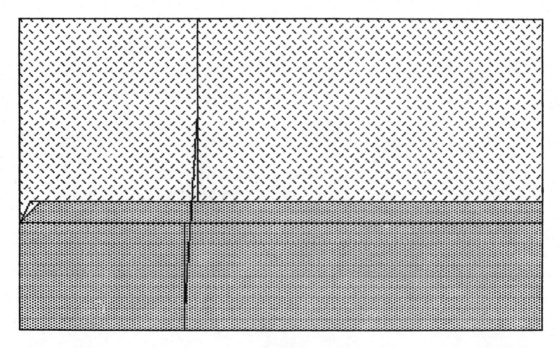

Fig. 2–8. In this close-up of a band, you can see that the cross-cut lines in two strips do not match exactly. To cut the segment, ease over from one cross-cut line to the other on the slanted line shown. The cut line should be as smooth as possible.

21

easier to keep track of where you are in the pattern. In addition, when segments are of different widths, the cross-cut lines will be marked in the order in which they occur in the pattern, so cutting only one segment at a time makes it easier to get the pattern right.

When you sew the strips together, the cross-cut lines provide ready-made guidelines for pinning. When you sew segments together, you might need to do some measuring. You do know that the ends of the segment should come out exactly even, and matching the ends might be all you need for short segments. In larger projects, you might need to measure and pin every foot or so along the way.

Sewing the segments together is, again, just straight quarter-inch seaming. Check to be sure that you're sewing in the right segment and that you haven't got it swapped end for end. Then as you sew over the seams within the segments simply let all the seam allowances fall toward you. This is their natural tendency, since they will be pushed toward you by the presser foot.

Chapter 3
Instructions for a Come-On Quilt

A Come-On quilt is made by constructing two different bands and then alternating segments from the two bands to make a pattern, as shown in Chapter 1. This chapter contains directions for a small quilt, which will be a good size for a baby quilt, a lap robe, or a wall hanging. I make many quilts about this size, since it's big enough to show off the pattern, but small enough to make quickly. I can make a quilt top this size in about 5 hours, from cutting the first fabric to finishing the border. Chapter 4 tells how to turn a quilt top into a finished quilt.

There are two variations of the Come-On quilt in this chapter. The piecing pattern is exactly the same for both, but the ways in which different fabrics are used make the versions look different. Also included are instructions for a smaller project, a set of Come-On place mats. There are two variations for the place mats: one with all the mats the same, and one made from scrap-bag fabrics, with each mat slightly different. Fig. C–1 in the color section shows a Scrapbag Come-On, and Fig. C–2 shows one of many variations of Come-On that you can do.

ARRANGING FABRICS WITHIN THE PATTERN

Figure 3–1 is a line drawing of the assembled Come-On quilt. Figures 3–2 through 3–5 show ways that fabrics could be arranged within the pattern.

The first version, shown in Fig. 3–2, is a Come-On made with only two fabrics. (See Table 3–1.) If you're going to buy fabric, you'll only need to make 2 choices for this one. Figure 3–3 shows a scrap-bag version, with a pattern area made from only a little of each of 12 fabrics. (See Table 3–2.) The small rectangles at the top and bottom of the pattern area have been cut from the fabric used for the border, creating the effect of a fringed edge to the pattern area. The version in Fig. 3–4 uses 7 fabrics shading out from the center. (See Table 3–3.) In all of these variations, the same fabric is used for the squares and rectangles in each horizontal row. Figure 3–5 diverges from this pattern: the rectangles have been grouped to form broad bands, and the fabrics used for the squares are different from those used for the rectangles. (See Table 3–4.)

Before you make a Come-On quilt, you'll probably want to make a mock-up of the design in color. Color a photocopy of Fig. 3–1 or lay tracing paper over the diagram in the book and color on the tracing paper. You can use crayons, felt markers, colored pencils, or anything else you like. Some quilters like to paste bits of fabric to a drawing, which, although time-consuming, gives a truer idea of the colors. Color in one of the arrangements shown, or invent a new Come-On version of your own. Just remember that Come-On is made with only two kinds of segments, so that if you color a square in blue, then you must use blue for all the other squares in that horizontal row.

If you're unsure of yourself, you might find yourself getting very involved in planning a quilt, and reluctant to start making it. You can be reassured by the fact that Come-On is a pattern that works well in almost any combination of colors. So, after you've colored a few drawings, go ahead and choose one, even if you don't think it's perfect. Pieced and repieced quilts have a way of surprising you, and I usually like my finished quilts better than the drawings.

PLANNING THE STRIPS

Look back at Figs. 1–1 through 1–4, which show how Come-On is made. Thirteen segments are cut from Band A, and 12 from Band B. Each segment is 1½ inches wide (1 inch, plus a quarter-inch seam allowance on either side), so that the strips in Band A must be 19½ inches long ($13 \times 1\frac{1}{2} = 19\frac{1}{2}$), and the strips in Band B must be 18 inches long ($12 \times 1\frac{1}{2} = 18$). The wide strips will finish 5 inches wide, and therefore must be cut 5½ inches wide. The narrow strips will finish 1 inch wide, so they must be cut 1½ inches wide. Finally, the smaller rectangles at the top and bottom edges of the pattern come from a strip of intermediate width cut 2½ inches wide. Tables 3–1 through 3–4 show the strips needed for the variations shown in Fig. 3–2 through 3–5, respectively.

For each fabric in the scrap-bag Come-On, you'll need two strips: one for Band A and one for Band B. For each fabric, simply read across the row in Table 3–2 to see the dimensions of the strips. For quilts like the two-fabric Come-On and the shaded Come-On, fabrics are repeated, so the tables specify the numbers of strips, as well as the dimensions of the strips.

Fig. 3 – 1. This line drawing shows all the seam lines in a completed Come-On quilt, and is used to plan the placement of colors in the quilt.

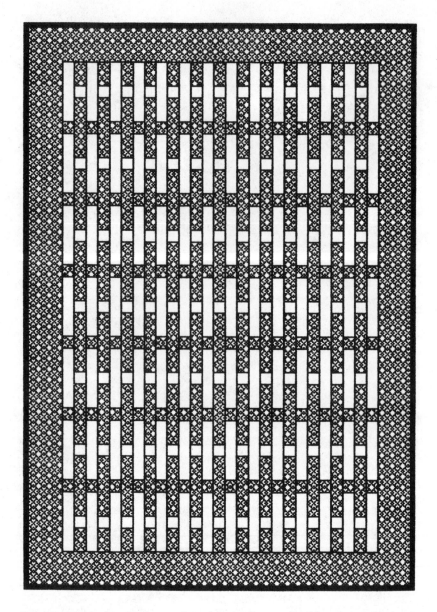

Fig. 3–2. This is the simplest version of Come-On, made with only two fabrics.

Table 3 – 1. Strips for Come-On with Two Fabrics.

GRID SIZE: **1**″ Finished Size of Pattern Area: **41**″ × **25**″

	BAND A (19 1/2″ strips)	BAND B (18″ strips)
Fabric 1		2 @ 2 1/2″ × 18″
	6 @ 1 1/2″ × 19 1/2″	6 @ 5 1/2″ × 18″
Fabric 2	7 @ 5 1/2″ × 19 1/2″	7 @ 1 1/2″ × 18″

SHOPPING LIST

Fabric 1: 1 1/2 yards 45″ wide fabric. Includes borders. Before you cut any strips, cut the fabric, along the lengthwise grain of the fabric, into two sections. The strips will be cut from one section, and the border will be cut from the other. The section for the strips should be about 20″ wide.

Fabric 2: 3/4 yard 45″ wide fabric.

Backing: 1 1/2 yards 45″ wide fabric. Enough fabric will be left over to use for binding.

Batting: Exact size depends on border width, but about 36″ × 54″.

Binding: About 4 2/3 yards of 1 1/2″ binding. Can be purchased, cut from extra backing fabric, or cut from 1/4 yard of another fabric.

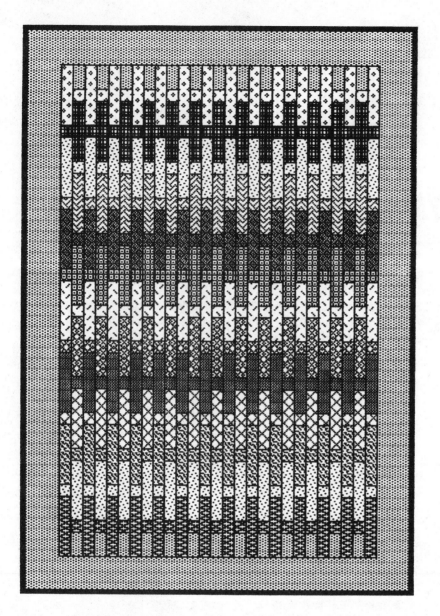

Fig. 3–3. This is the scrap-bag version of Come-On. Each row of the pattern is made from a different fabric. The pieces at the top and bottom ends of the pattern area have been made to match the border.

Table 3 – 2. Strips for Scrap-Bag Come-On.

GRID SIZE: **1**″ Finished Size of Pattern Area: **41″ × 25″**

	BAND A (19 1/2″ strips)	BAND B (18″ strips)
Fabric 1		2 @ 2 1/2″ × 18″
Fabric 2	5 1/2″ × 19 1/2″	1 1/2″ × 18″
Fabric 3	1 1/2″ × 19 1/2″	5 1/2″ × 18″
Fabric 4	5 1/2″ × 19 1/2″	1 1/2″ × 18″
Fabric 5	1 1/2″ × 19 1/2″	5 1/2″ × 18″
Fabric 6	5 1/2″ × 19 1/2″	1 1/2″ × 18″
Fabric 7	1 1/2″ × 19 1/2″	5 1/2″ × 18″
Fabric 8	5 1/2″ × 19 1/2″	1 1/2″ × 18″
Fabric 9	1 1/2″ × 19 1/2″	5 1/2″ × 18″
Fabric 10	5 1/2″ × 19 1/2″	1 1/2″ × 18″
Fabric 11	1 1/2″ × 19 1/2″	5 1/2″ × 18″
Fabric 12	5 1/2″ × 19 1/2″	1 1/2″ × 18″

SHOPPING LIST

Fabric 1: 1 1/2 yards 45″ wide fabric. Cut the two strips across the width of the fabric. The remaining fabric will be used for the border, with enough left over for the binding.

Fabrics 2-12: Scraps large enough to cut strips indicated, or 1/4 yard of each.

Backing: 1 1/2 yards 45″ wide fabric. Enough fabric will be left over to use for binding.

Batting: Exact size depends on border width, but about 36″ × 54″.

Binding: About 4 2/3 yards of 1 1/2″ binding. Can be purchased, cut from extra border or backing fabric, or cut from 1/4 yard of another fabric.

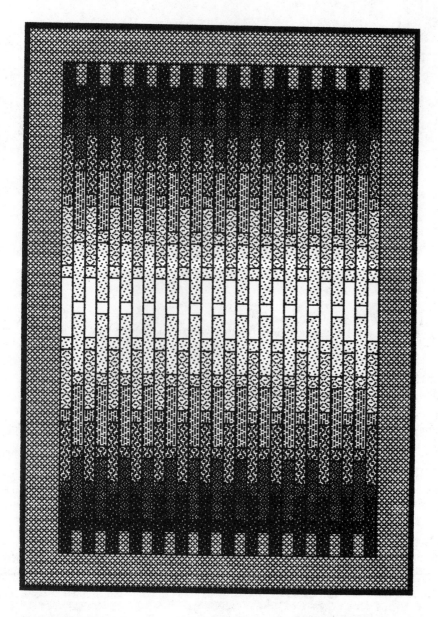

Fig. 3–4. The shaded Come-On uses a light fabric for the center row, and darker and darker fabrics for outer rows. The end pieces match the border.

Table 3–3. Strips for Shaded Come-On.

GRID SIZE: **1**″ Finished Size of Pattern Area: **41**″ × **25**″

	BAND A (19 1/2″ strips)	BAND B (18″ strips)
Fabric 1		2 @ 2 1/2″ × 18″
Fabric 2	2 @ 5 1/2″ × 19 1/2″	2 @ 1 1/2″ × 18″
Fabric 3	2 @ 1 1/2″ × 19 1/2″	2 @ 5 1/2″ × 18″
Fabric 4	2 @ 5 1/2″ × 19 1/2″	2 @ 1 1/2″ × 18″
Fabric 5	2 @ 1 1/2″ × 19 1/2″	2 @ 5 1/2″ × 18″
Fabric 6	2 @ 5 1/2″ × 19 1/2″	2 @ 1 1/2″ × 18″
Fabric 7	2 @ 1 1/2″ × 19 1/2″	2 @ 5 1/2″ × 18″
Fabric 8	1 @ 5 1/2″ × 19 1/2″	1 @ 1 1/2″ × 18″

SHOPPING LIST

Fabric 1: 1 1/2 yards 45″ wide fabric. Cut the two strips across the width of the fabric. The remaining fabric will be used for the border, with enough left over for the binding.

Fabrics 2-8: 1/4 yard 45″ fabric for each.

Backing: 1 1/2 yards 45″ wide fabric. Enough fabric will be left over to use for binding.

Batting: Exact size depends on border width, but about 36″ × 54″.

Binding: About 4 2/3 yards of 1 1/2″ binding. Can be purchased, or cut from extra border or backing fabric, or from 1/4 yard of another fabric.

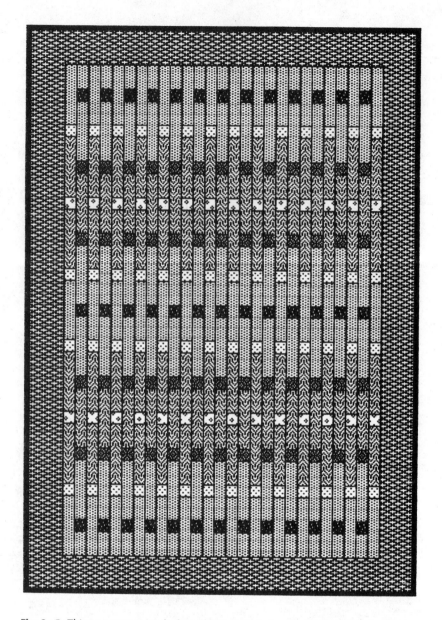

Fig. 3–5. This pattern was made from the same line drawing as the other Come-On quilts, but the colors have not been arranged to form the same kinds of rows of patterns as in the others. Like the shaded Come-On, this pattern is symmetrical from top to bottom.

Table 3–4. Strips for Broad-Band Come-On.

GRID SIZE: **1**″ Finished Size of Pattern Area: **41**″ × **25**″

	BAND A (19 1/2″ strips)	BAND B (18″ strips)
Fabric 1	3 @ 5 1/2″ × 19 1/2″	2 @ 2 1/2″ × 18″
Fabric 2		3 @ 1 1/2″ × 18″
Fabric 3	4 @ 1 1/2″ × 19 1/2″	
Fabric 4	4 @ 5 1/2″ × 19 1/2″	7 @ 5 1/2″ × 18″
Fabric 5		4 @ 1 1/2″ × 18″
Fabric 6	2 @ 1 1/2″ × 19 1/2″	

SHOPPING LIST

Fabric 1: 5/8 yard 45″ wide fabric

Fabric 2: 1/8 yard 45″ wide fabric

Fabric 3: 1/8 yard 45″ wide fabric

Fabric 4: 1 yard 45″ wide fabric

Fabric 5: 1/8 yard 45″ wide fabric

Fabric 6: 1/8 yard 45″ wide fabric

Border: 1 1/2 yards 36″ or 45″ wide fabric. Enough fabric will be left over to use for binding.

Backing: 1 1/2 yards 45″ wide fabric. Enough fabric will be left over to use for binding.

Batting: Exact size depends on border width, but about 36″ × 54″.

Binding: About 4 2/3 yards of 1 1/2″ binding. Can be purchased, cut from extra border or backing fabric, or cut from 1/4 yard of another fabric.

CONSTRUCTING THE QUILT

Following the directions in Chapter 2, cut all the stripping you'll need. All the segments in the Come-On quilt are 1½ inches wide, so you'll need a paper template at least 19½ inches long with marks every 1½ inches. Mark the cross-cut lines on the strips, and sew Band A and Band B.

Cut a segment from Band A and a segment from Band B, and place the Band B segment on top of the Band A segment, right sides together. If you're doing the scrap-bag version of Come-On, check to be sure that you don't have one of the segments flipped end for end. In the other versions, both ends are the same. The distance between a seam in one segment and the next seam in the other segment should be 2 inches. Pin the segments together at the ends and at as many other places as you like, then sew the segments together.

After you have sewn the first two segments together, cut another segment from Band A. Lay it, face down, on top of the Band B segment already sewn into the pattern area. Figure 3 – 6 shows how the left-hand edge of the second Band A segment lies on top of the first Band A segment. Since these two segments from the same band should line up, you can use the segment already in place to help you place the second segment, or you can measure and pin as before.

Continue in this manner, cutting alternate segments from Bands A and B and sewing them to the pattern area. When you're done, press the pattern area. All the little seam allowances within the segments already will be lying in one direction. It doesn't matter in which direction you press the long seam allowances, but you should press all of them the same way.

Now that the pattern area is done and pressed, pin it up on a wall so that you can back off and take a look at it. You'll probably find that it didn't turn out quite the way you visualized it, but you might find it looks better than you expected. If you're not completely happy with the pattern, try to figure out why. Because piecing and repiecing is relatively fast, a disappointment with the pattern is not a complete disaster. You can try again, with another choice of fabrics. It's certainly not worthwhile to disassemble what you've done. More than likely, however, you'll find that your Come-On is successful in its own unique way, and you'll want to go ahead and make it into a quilt.

If you have not already chosen the border fabric, try each possible fabric out against the pattern area. Unfold the fabric and pin it up on a wall or lay it out flat on a table or the floor, right side up. Lay the pattern area on top of the fabric you're considering for the border, with about 4 inches of the border fabric showing around a corner of the pattern area. Step back and look at that corner. Try out all the fabrics in this way, and choose your favorite.

I suggest a 3- to 5-inch border, but choose the border width that looks good on your particular quilt. Again, place a corner of the quilt on the border fabric, and step back to consider. Does the border seem overwhelming, or meager, or just right? Adjust the placement until you're satisfied. If you're a little undecided, cut the border a little on the wide side, since you can trim it after you sew it in place, but if it looks skimpy, you can't add any. Remember that you'll need to cut the border pieces ½ inch wider than the finished width you decide on, to allow for seam allowances.

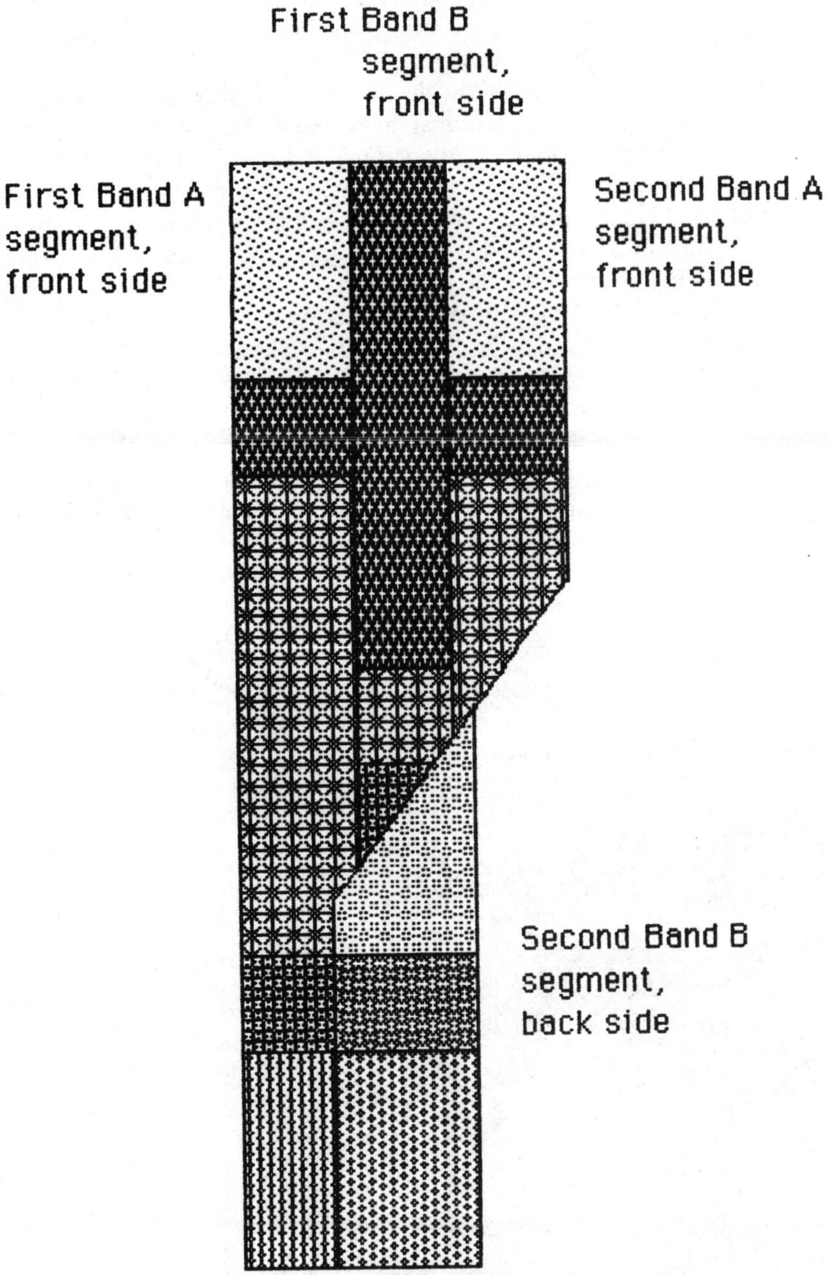

First Band B
segment,
front side

First Band A
segment,
front side

Second Band A
segment,
front side

Second Band B
segment,
back side

Fig. 3–6. This illustration shows how the third segment of a Come-On quilt matches up with the first segment. The top part of the segment has been opened out, and shows how the segment looks in the finished pattern area. The lower part shows how the segment is placed while it is being sewn. Notice how the seam lines on the back of the third segment line up with those on the front of the first segment. Matching these seam lines is sometimes easier than measuring the placement of the third segment against the second segment.

35

Following the directions in Chapter 4, add the border to your pattern area, then baste the quilt top to the backing and batting. The following quilting designs, whether for hand or machine quilting, do not require marking.

The heavy lines in Fig. 3–7 show the corner of a Come-On quilt with a simple machine-quilting pattern. The pattern area is quilted along the long seams between segments, a method called *quilting in the ditch.* A line of quilting runs around the pattern area, in the ditch. Three lines of quilting run around the border. The first runs around the border ¼ inch from the first. The outermost line runs around the outside of the quilt ½ inch from the raw edge of the border fabric, which will be ¼ inch from the edge of the binding when that has been sewn on. The last line quilted runs up the middle of the border, halfway between the other two.

Simple patterns for hand quilting Come-On quilts are shown in Figs. 3–8 and 3–9. Quilting lines, indicated in the diagrams by heavy lines, follow the edges of the fabric areas. All quilting lines that parallel piecing lines are ¼ inch from the seams and so need not be marked before quilting. You can judge the distance between quilting line and seams by eye, or you can use ¼-inch-wide masking tape as a guide. In each of these patterns, lay out the quilting lines in the border like those in the machine-quilting pattern.

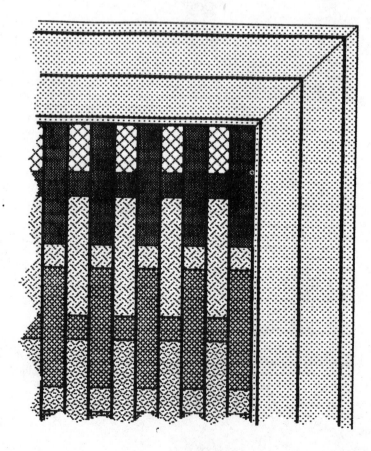

Fig. 3–7. The heavy lines show the position of machine-quilting lines. The pattern area is quilted *in the ditch,* or along seam lines.

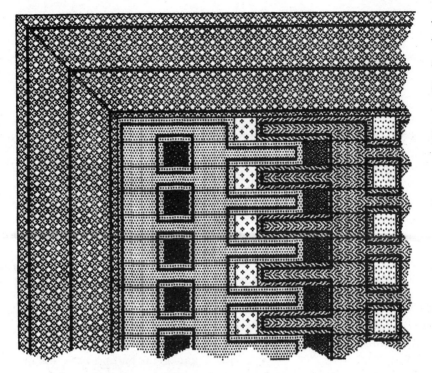

Fig. 3 – 9. The heavy lines show the position of hand-quilting lines for the broad-band Come-On variation.

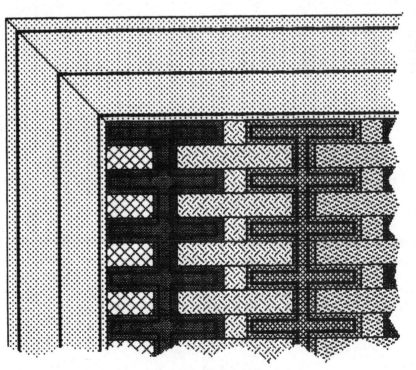

Fig. 3 – 8. The heavy lines show the position of hand-quilting lines for a scrap-bag Come-On quilt. The same design can be used for the two-color Come-On.

37

COME-ON PLACE MATS

Figures 3–10 and 3–11 show two kinds of Come-On place mats. The first uses four fabrics in a symmetrical arrangement, with the fourth fabric used for the border. (See Table 3–5.) All place mats in a set will be the same, so four fabrics are sufficient for the whole set. The instructions call for strips 54 or 48 inches long, which is, of course, longer than can be cut across the width of most fabrics. You can make the strips by getting as much as possible from one width of the fabric, then piecing out the rest, or you can cut twice as many strips half as long (27 and 24 inches long), which might be easier.

The variation shown in Fig. 3–11 uses seven different fabrics in each place mat, not counting the border fabric. (See Table 3–6.) Each mat will be made with different fabrics, so that up to 28 scrap fabrics can be used in a set of four place mats. The fabrics are described as "light" or "dark." Using light and dark fabrics is an old scrap-quilt trick for imposing order on chaos. It is not necessary to have 28 completely different fabrics. You could repeat a few fabrics, or you could use one fabric heavily to give further unity to the set. An extreme example of repetition within the scrap-bag context would be the use of muslin for all the "light" fabrics or a single dark fabric for all the "dark" fabrics.

After you have completed the place-mat pattern areas, add 1½-inch border strips, which will give 1-inch finished borders. Decide whether you want batting in the place mats. Use batting if you want a soft effect, or if you want to quilt the place mats. Place mats without batting need not be quilted. If you do use batting, use something lightweight. Possibilities include nonwoven fleece, which is like very thin batting, or a layer of flannel or some other soft fabric.

You can construct place mats (with or without batting) like miniature quilts, complete with binding, or you can make them by the *pillow method*. For the pillow method, lay the front and back of a place mat right sides together, as shown in Fig. 3–12, sew, then turn right side out. The pillow method works well only with small pieces like place mats. If the edges of a large quilt are sewn together in this way, it's almost impossible to get the layers to lie completely flat.

If you decide on the pillow method, measure the place mat, then cut the backing to the size of the place mat. Place the front on the backing with right sides together. If you are using batting, place the batting on top of the front. Pin the layers together and sew most of the way around, using a quarter-inch seam allowance and leaving a 3- or 4-inch space for turning. Trim the corners. If you've used batting, trim it very close to the seam.

Turn the place mat right side out, and pull out the corners. Baste the turning space closed. You must fold the edges of the place mat exactly along the seam line between the top and the backing, so the place mat will lie flat. If you haven't used batting, then press the edges with an iron. If you have used batting (which could melt with the heat of an iron), finger-press, then baste around the edge. Stitch around the edges to keep them permanently in place through washing and handling. Add further quilting if desired.

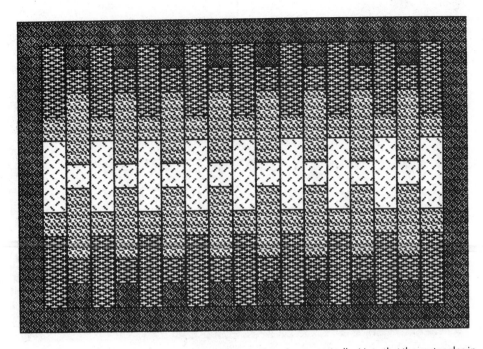

Fig. 3‑10. The fabrics in this Come-On place mat are placed symmetrically. Note that the rectangles in the Come-On place mats are 1 × 3 inches, rather than 1 × 5 inches, as in the Come-On quilt.

Table 3‑5. Strips for Set of Four Symmetrical Come-On Place Mats.

GRID SIZE: **1**″ Finished Size of Pattern Area: **11**″ × **17**″

	BAND A (54″ strips)	BAND B (48″ strips)
Fabric 1		2 @ 1 1/2″ × 48″
Fabric 2	2 @ 3 1/2″ × 54″	2 @ 1 1/2″ × 48″
Fabric 3	2 @ 1 1/2″ × 54″	2 @ 3 1/2″ × 48″
Fabric 4	1 @ 3 1/2″ × 54″	1 @ 1 1/2″ × 48″

SHOPPING LIST

Fabric 1: 3/4 yard 45″ wide fabric. Cut the strips from across the width of the fabric. The remainder of the fabric will be used for the borders.

Fabric 2: 3/8 yard 45″ wide fabric.

Fabric 3: 3/8 yard 45″ wide fabric.

Fabric 4: 1/4 yard 45″ wide fabric.

Backing: 7/8 yard 45″ wide fabric.

Batting: (optional)Four pieces, each about 16″ × 22″.

Binding: About 7 1/4 yards. Use 1″ binding if not using batting; use 1 1/2″ binding if using batting. Can be purchased or cut from 3/8 yard of 45″ fabric.

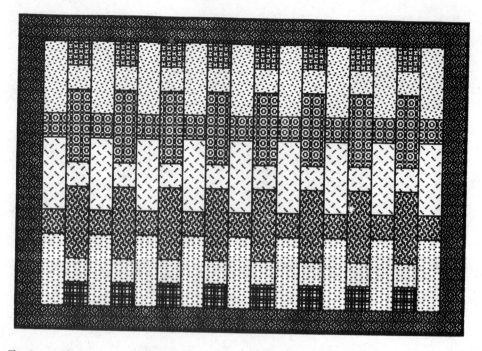

Fig. 3–11. This is a scrap-bag arrangement for the Come-On place mat. All place mats in a set of scrap-bag place mats could be the same, or each could be different.

Table 3–6. Strips for a Set of Four Scrap-Bag Come-On Place Mats.

GRID SIZE: **1**″ Finished Size of Pattern Area: **11**″ × **17**″

	BAND A **(13 1/2″ strips)**	BAND B **(12″ strips)**
Each of 12 light fabrics	1 @ 3 1/2″ × 13 1/2″	1 @ 1 1/2″ × 12″
Each of 8 dark fabrics	1 @ 1 1/2″ × 13 1/2″	1 @ 3 1/2″ × 12″
Each of 8 dark fabrics		1 @ 1 1/2″ × 12″

SHOPPING LIST

Fabrics: Scraps, or 1/4 yard for each.

Border: 5/8 yard 45″ wide fabric.

Backing: 7/8 yard 45″ wide fabric.

Batting: (optional) Four pieces, each about 16″ × 22″.

Binding: About 7 1/4 yards. Use 1″ binding if not using batting; use 1 1/2″ binding if using batting. Can be purchased or cut from 3/8 yard of 45″ fabric.

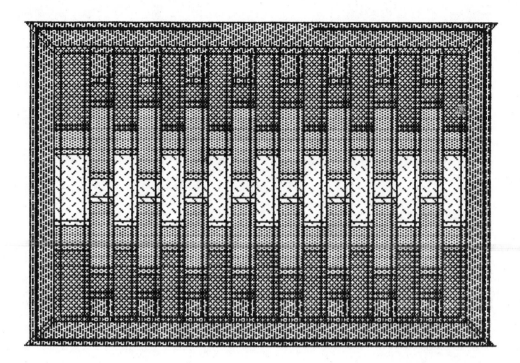

Fig. 3 – 12. This is the back side of the top for a Come-On place mat. Note how all seam allowances in the pattern area have been pressed down or to the right. The dark line around the outside shows the sewing line for finishing this place mat by the pillow method. The place mat top is sewn to the back and batting along this line, then the place mat is turned right side out through the opening at the top.

Chapter 4

Turning a Quilt Top into a Quilt

When your pieced and repieced pattern is finished, you're about halfway to a finished quilt. When the border has been added, the quilt top will be done. The next step is to choose the backing and the batting. Before basting the layers together, choose the quilting pattern. If the quilting pattern requires marking, it will be easier to mark it before basting the top to the batting and the backing.

Quilting is the process of sewing the layers of the quilt together, and can be done by hand or by machine. Hand quilting usually requires a hoop or frame. Machine quilting might require a special presser foot or attachment for your sewing machine. Machine quilting is faster than hand quilting, but it is also trickier, since the layers of the quilt will try to slip around as the quilt is handled. The sheer work of maneuvering a quilt through the sewing machine, especially a big quilt, also can be a problem.

When the quilting is done, the edge is covered with binding. I use bias binding, which can be purchased or made from scratch. Finally, your quilt deserves to be signed.

BORDERS

Most quilts look better with a border. For some quilts, the narrow line created by the binding might be enough, but most need a wider frame around the pattern area.

You figured out how big the pattern area should be when you planned the pattern, but you should measure the pattern area to be sure it is that size. The natural way to measure the pattern area is to stretch a measuring tape along its edges. Unfortunately, the edge can be stretched more easily than the rest of the pattern area, so it's safer to measure right across the middle of the pattern area. Even the middle of the quilt can be stretched, but measuring there will be more accurate than measuring along the edge.

Remember that when you measure the pattern area, from fabric edge to fabric edge, the measurement you get is ½ inch larger than the size the pattern area will be in the finished quilt because of the quarter-inch seam allowance on each edge of the pattern area. I'll refer to the edge-to-edge measurement as the *full length* (or width) of the pattern area. The *finished length* or width of the pattern area is ½ inch less.

I usually cut the borders on the lengthwise grain of the fabric, partly to get long border pieces and partly to avoid the stretchiness of strips cut on the crosswise grain. However, sometimes I do cut borders on the crosswise grain of the fabric when I have only a little fabric or when I want the effect I'll achieve by cutting a stripe or another pattern on the crosswise grain.

Trim off the selvage of the fabric before you cut the borders. Selvages might look like neatly prefinished edges, but they are usually more tightly woven than the rest of the fabric, and might distort the edge or give an inaccurate measurement.

Start by cutting strips of border fabric that are the right width, but longer than needed. The length you need depends on the way the corners of the border are treated. There are two basic ways to treat the corner of a border. The easier corner to sew is the abutted corner, shown in Fig. 4–1. The mitered corner shown in Fig. 4–2 is more difficult to sew because of the angled seam. A mitered border is more satisfactory when the seam will show up clearly, as it will with solid fabrics or with fabrics with regularly repeating patterns. Mitered borders also take more fabric than abutted borders.

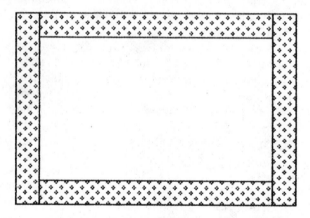

Fig. 4–1. These border pieces have been sewn on the pattern area with abutted corners.

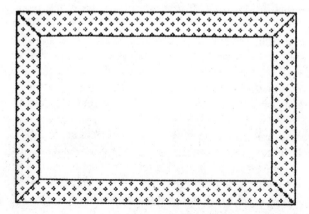

Fig. 4–2. The corners of these border pieces have been joined with miters.

44

With either type of corner, the borders are sewn to the pattern area with a simple quarter-inch seam. When you're ready to sew this seam, put the pattern area and border on the sewing machine, in place for sewing, with the pattern area on top. If the seam allowances in the pattern area are laid over toward the sewing machine, the seam will be hard to sew, so flip the whole piece over so that the border piece is on top. You'll find that two border-to-pattern area seams will be sewn with the border fabric on top, and two with the pattern area on top.

Abutted Corners

Abutted borders often work well with big, splashy patterns, but you might want to spend some time checking to be sure that the seams where the border pieces meet really won't be obtrusive. Cut out the pieces of stripping you'll use for border and place them around the pattern area to check that a seam will not cut right through a prominent motif, like a big, red rose. Try rearranging the border pieces until you find a satisfactory arrangement.

I'll assume that you're adding the borders to the long sides first. The rectangles for these first two borders are cut to the full length of the pattern area. Sew these first two borders in place with a quarter-inch seam. Find the length of the second border by measuring across the pattern area and the two borders already in place, from fabric edge to fabric edge. Cut the second pair of borders to this length and sew them in place.

Mitered Corners

For a mitered border, you'll need two strips of border fabric at least as long as the full length of the quilt top, and two strips of border fabric at least as long as the full width of the quilt top. The full length of the quilt top will be the full length of the pattern area plus twice the finished width of the border. The full width of the quilt top will be the full width of the pattern area plus twice the finished width of the border.

The next step is to measure and mark the seam lines for the mitered corners on each border piece. Figures 4–3 through 4–6 show the steps you'll follow. Mark one of the long borders first. The point at which the mark and the line segment intersect, the *corner point,* is the place at which the angled miter seam will meet the seam that connects the border to the pattern area.

Mark corner points on the back of the pattern area ¼ inch in from each edge. Choose the edge of the pattern area to which you will sew a border first. With the appropriate piece on top, match and pin the corner points on the border to the corner points on the pattern area, then pin at several places between the corners. You'll sew the border pieces to the pattern area with the usual quarter-inch seam, but sew only between the corner points. You don't want the stitching to run beyond the corner points, because it then would interfere with sewing on the other border piece that will be connected at that point. To secure the ends of the seam, start and end with about ½ inch of backstitching.

Sew on the other three borders in the same way as the first. At this point, the borders are attached to the pattern area, but the ends of the border strips are loose at the corners of the quilt. However, you already have marked all the seam lines for the miter seams, so sewing these seams will not be difficult.

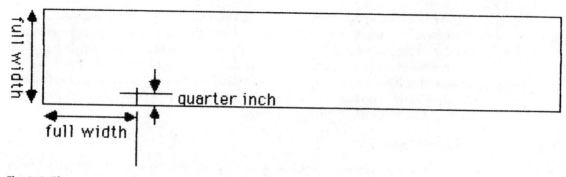

Fig. 4–3. The corner point for the mitered corner is ¼ inch from the edge of the border. The distance from the end of the border piece to the corner point is the same as the full width of the border piece.

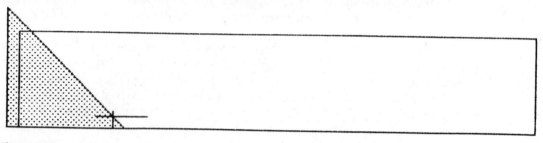

Fig. 4–4. A triangle has been placed so that one edge lines up with the edge of the border piece, while the angled side passes through the corner point. Draw along the angled side of the triangle to mark the miter line.

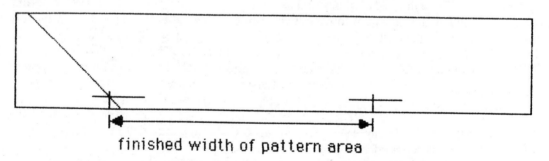

Fig. 4–5. The distance from the first corner point to the corner point at the other end of the border piece is the same as the finished width of the pattern area.

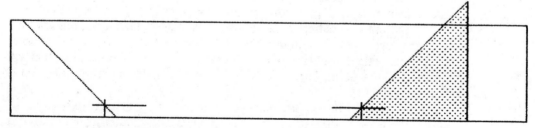

Fig. 4–6. The second miter line is marked with a triangle. Again, place the triangle with one side on the edge of the border piece so that the slanted side passes through the corner point.

Choose a corner and fold the quilt top, right sides in, as shown in Fig. 4–7. Match the miter seam lines marked on the two border pieces. Stick pins through the miter line on the top border piece. Turn the quilt over and check that the pins have come out on the miter line on the back border piece. If necessary, adjust them so that they do. The outside edges of the borders also should match up. At the corner point, fold the seam allowances from the border-to-pattern-area seam toward the pattern area, so that they'll be out of your way as you sew the miter seam. Backstitch up to the corner point along the miter line, then stitch along the miter line to the edge of the border. Open out the miter to check that the mitered corner lies flat, then trim off the ends of the border strips ¼ inch outside the miter line. Sew the other three mitered corners.

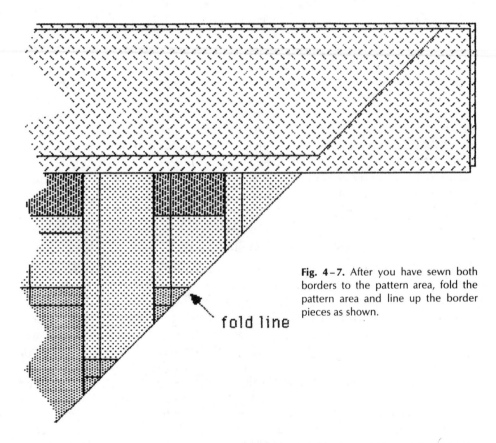

fold line

Fig. 4–7. After you have sewn both borders to the pattern area, fold the pattern area and line up the border pieces as shown.

BACKING

The quilt back is usually pretty simple. The backing should be bigger than the quilt top by at least 4 inches in each direction to allow for 2 inches extra on each side. The extra allows for the tendency of the layers to slip around some while you're working with them. For small projects, such as place mats, only about 1 inch extra on each edge is needed.

Choose a fabric that goes with the quilt top and is similar in weight to the fabrics in the quilt top. For large quilts, you usually must piece the backing. Sew two or three lengths of fabric together for the back after you trim the selvages off. If you decide to use a sheet for your backing, choose a cheaper muslin sheet rather than a more expensive percale sheet, since it will be easier to quilt through.

BATTING

Throughout most of their history, most quilts were made with cotton batting. Cotton batting is still available but must be quilted with lines no more than 1 inch apart to prevent the batting from lumping up when the quilt is washed. I generally use polyester batting, of which there are several varieties.

Batts vary in thickness and in the extent to which the polyester fibers have been bound together. Batting is a highly personal choice, and each expert prefers a certain kind, so you might want to experiment to find the kind you like best. I've used several kinds, but have settled on the one that's most easily available at my local fabric store.

The batting, like the quilt back, should be big enough to allow for 2 inches extra on all sides of the quilt top. If you buy batting by the yard or if you're using leftover pieces, you might need to piece it. You can piece batting together quite easily by laying the pieces down, side by side, with the edges touching. I find the batting usually sticks to the backing and I don't need to do anything more. If the batting seems likely to slip, gently whip the two edges together with sewing thread. The whipping stitches need not be close and should be left rather loose.

MARKING THE QUILTING PATTERN

Some quilting patterns simply follow the piecing lines of the quilt top, and for these patterns no marking is necessary. You can mark other patterns with masking tape. For others, you must draw the pattern on the fabric with a marker of some kind.

Masking tape is suitable for patterns composed of straight lines. Place the tape on the quilt and sew along the edge of the tape. Quilt shops often carry ¼-inch-wide masking tape, which is useful for quilting ¼ inch from a seam. Place one edge on the seam, then quilt along the other edge. I understand that ¼-inch masking tape also is used for painting stripes on cars, so an auto supply store also might carry it. Check your masking tape to be sure that no adhesive remains on the quilt. If you leave the quilting for any length of time, remove the tape from the quilt.

If marking the design is necessary, you should use something whose marks can be removed. Chalk, dressmaker's chalk, and soap are the old standbys. Wash-out pencils will work too, if they truly wash out. As I've mentioned, I'm wary of the disappearing markers.

I don't use pencil for marking quilting designs although pencil lines are still visible on some museum quilts made 200 years ago. My objection is that these lines are still visible. It bothers me to see the marking lines on a quilt. I've heard about various methods of getting rid of pencil lines, and even tried some, but didn't find them satisfactory.

Because chalk, soap, and wash-out pencils tend to rub off the fabric as the quilt is handled, you need to consider when to mark the quilt. If you mark before basting, you will need to handle the quilt gently, and might need to refresh the markings as you work. If you wait until after you baste the quilt, the softness of the quilt sandwich makes accurate marking difficult. For intricate designs, I mark the quilt top before I baste the quilt, since I need a hard surface for detail marking. Most of the time, I use designs that can be marked as I go, or that do not require much precision in the marking and can be marked after basting.

BASTING

You will need to baste the three layers of a quilt unless you're using an old-fashioned quilting frame that holds a whole quilt stretched flat. The biggest problem with basting is finding a place to baste. I baste on a table whenever I can, but often the only big enough surface is the floor. Even finding a floor big enough might be a problem. I have found uncarpeted floors at friends' houses, in churches, or at work on a Saturday. Unfortunately, basting on the floor means a lot of crawling and kneeling, and is hard on the knees and the back. You might be able to find someone with a ping-pong table, or a school or church with several tables that could be pushed together.

Once you have a place, spread out the backing with the seam allowances on top, so that they will end up inside the quilt. To keep the backing flat while you lay out the other layers of the quilt, stick the backing to the floor or table with masking tape. Test, of course, to be sure the tape won't damage the surface to which you're sticking. The backing should be smooth, but not taut. An absence of wrinkles is all that's really needed. If you happen to be working on a flooring with a rectangular pattern in it, the lines in the flooring can assist you in seeing that the backing is square.

After you have secured the backing, lay out the batting. This is the point at which you will piece your batting, if necessary. Then add the quilt top, face up, leaving margins of batting and backing all around the quilt top. Smooth the quilt top out, and check that it's more or less squared up with the backing.

Pin all around the edge of the quilt with straight pins. Then baste a grid over the quilt, in 6- to 8-inch squares, including lines of basting right at the edges of the quilt top. The basting stitches should be big, one stitch every 2 or 3 inches. After you have finished basting, remove the masking tape and the pins around the edge.

QUILTING

Hand quilting is traditional, gives a softer quilted line, and can be used for more intricate patterns. For smaller projects, it's also portable. Hand quilting is, however, more time-consuming than machine quilting and usually requires a frame or a hoop.

Machine quilting is much faster than hand quilting, gives a sharper line, but is usually suitable only for straight lines and gentle curves. Machine quilting a large quilt also means a lot of hoisting and shoving, and requires setting up a couple of tables around your machine, in position to bear the weight of the quilt. If you're not comfortable with your sewing machine, machine quilting might be more difficult than hand quilting.

Equipment for Hand Quilting: Frames and Hoops

Most hand quilters like to use something to hold the quilt taut while they quilt on it. Many use a quilting hoop, an oversize version of the embroidery hoop. Some use a hoop alone; others buy an oval hoop that comes on a floor stand. The stand takes some of the weight of the quilt off the quilter, in addition to providing stability.

A quilting frame provides a bigger working area than a hoop. Shifting a quilt about when you are using a hoop might lead to some shifting and wrinkling, but these problems are less likely with a frame. My mother does hybrid quilting. She does a minimum job on a frame, quilting just enough to get the quilt stabilized, then switches to a hoop.

Figure 4–8 shows the type of frame most commonly used today. It is as wide as the quilt, but has rollers at the front and back, so it is only 2 to 3 feet deep. You start quilting at one end of the quilt, quilt as far as you can reach comfortably, then roll a new portion of the quilt into position. Rolling frames are moderately expensive. If you have an experienced woodworker on tap, you might be able to get him to make you a quilting frame. Plans and the metal ratchets needed for the rollers are advertised in quilting magazines. Many roller frames can be tilted, and some people find this feature provides a more comfortable working position.

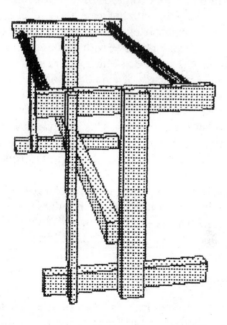

Fig. 4–8. A roller frame has two long dowels around which the quilt is wrapped. The rollers fit into side bars and, once rolled to the proper position, are kept in place with ratchets. Not shown here are the *aprons,* long strips of cloth stapled to the rollers to which the quilt is pinned. The legs and braces serve only to hold the frame steady at the right height.

An old-fashioned quilting frame, like that shown in Fig. 4–9, is a simpler device, easy to put together, and cheaper. It is simply four sticks, held together at the corners, to which the quilt is tacked or pinned. The frame is supported on chairs, on saw-horses, or on special stands, or is hung from the ceiling.

The disadvantage of the old-fashioned quilting frame is that it must be at least as big as the quilt being quilted. I have an old-fashioned quilting frame, but I use it only for quilting bees or for quilting demonstrations at public places.

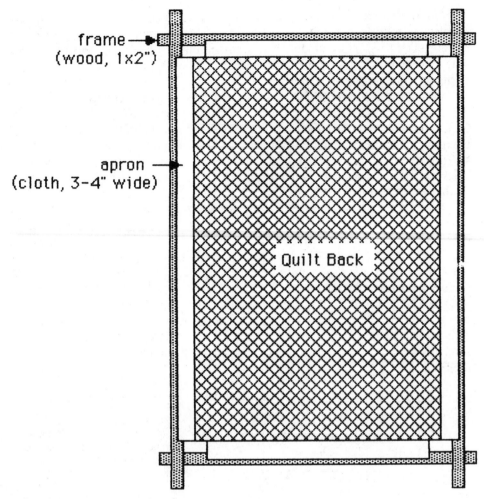

frame —→
(wood, 1x2")

apron —→
(cloth, 3-4" wide)

Quilt Back

Fig. 4 – 9. The frame part of an old-fashioned quilting frame consists of four sticks with aprons, which are held together at the corners with clamps or nails.

Hand Quilting

The hand-quilting stitch is a simple running stitch. The stitches need to go through all three layers of the quilt, and should be tight enough to create a valley in the quilt surface, but not so tight that they wrinkle the quilt. Also, the places where a thread begins and ends should be invisible, or at least obscured. Each quilter has her own opinions about the proper methods for achieving these goals, and mine are presented here.

Hand quilting is done with *quilting thread,* which is heavier than regular sewing thread, and has a slick finish that makes it easier than regular thread to pull through the thickness of a quilt. It comes in a limited range of colors, but since each quilting stitch nestles in its own shadowy recess, it's amazing how well the thread color blends in to the fabric.

Quilting needles are short needles with small eyes. You can use other types of needles for quilting, but quilting needles are especially appropriate for the rocking method of quilting. You can sometimes find quilting needles in tiny sizes, only 1 inch long, but the more commonly available size 8 or 9 needles are just fine, unless you're trying to set records for tiny stitches.

I usually start by tying a knot in my thread, then bringing the needle up from the back of the quilt to a place where I want to quilt. The next step gets the knot from the back of the quilt to the inside of the quilt. With the thread pulled taut from the front of the quilt, pinch the back of the quilt near the knot, and pull down, as shown in Fig. 4–10. You should hear a small pop as the knot is pulled inside the quilt. You might need to try a smaller knot if it won't pop through the backing, or a larger knot if it pops all the way through the quilt.

With some patterns, it's possible to start a quilting thread in the middle of the thread. Cut a double-length thread, take one stitch, then pull the ends of the thread even. Continue stitching with the end that is threaded in the needle. When that half of the thread is ended, go back to the end that was left hanging, and stitch with it.

The hardest thing about quilting stitches is getting the needle back up through all those layers without taking a huge stitch. Don't expect tiny stitches at first: a beginner is doing pretty well to get three or four stitches per inch (counting stitches on top only). Some people get frustrated by not being able to get small stitches with the running stitch and resort to the slower stab stitch, making each stitch up and each stitch down separately. Unfortunately, stab stitching often makes an uneven line on the back side.

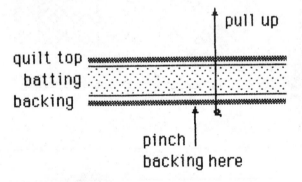

Fig. 4–10. This cross section of a quilt sandwich shows a knot ready to be pulled through the quilt back so that it will be hidden inside the quilt.

To get small running stitches, you will need to bend the cloth, since the needle is straight. When I feel the stitch coming through to the back, I push up on the needle at a point near the tip, then push the needle on through to the front, as shown in Fig. 4–11. There's quite a little mountain in the quilt as I'm pushing up. The hand under the quilt does most of the work, with the hand on top providing only the push.

You can quilt with the needle held in the usual way, grasped with thumb and forefinger. However, the "rocking method" is faster, and I find that the key to the rocking method is the way the needle is held. After the first stitch is placed, the needle is not "held" at all, merely pushed with the thimble, as shown in Fig. 4–12. The thimble gives greater leverage on the needle, which can be moved to steeper angles while quilting, so that it appears to "rock."

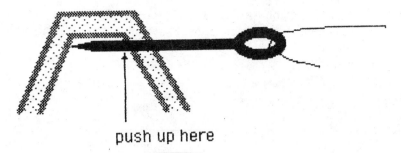

push up here

Fig. 4–11. This exaggerated cross section shows where the finger underneath the quilt pushes up on the quilt. The needle then acts as a lever with the under-side finger as its fulcrum, and the needle can be brought back up through the quilt.

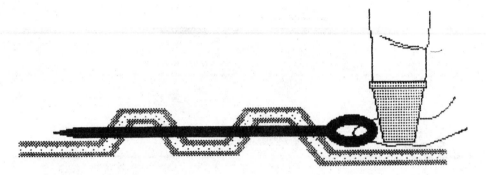

Fig. 4–12. This exaggerated cross section shows the position of the thimble finger. The side of the thimble pushes the needle through the quilt.

I try to end threads near a seam in the quilt top. If I'm not actually on a seam, I run the thread along inside the quilt to a seam. I take a couple of backstitches, hidden in the seam as well as possible, then take a long stitch inside the quilt. The tail end of the thread might be short enough to stay inside the quilt, but if it emerges, pull it tight and snip it off close to the quilt.

If you're quilting in a large, plain area, with no seams in sight, you might be able to take a couple of unobtrusive backstitches on top of your last quilting stitch, and then lose the thread. However, in a really wide-open spot, any backstitches might look awful. You might be able to bury the end of the thread inside the quilt as shown in Fig. 4–13. Turning the needle end for end in this way twists the thread in the batting, but doesn't make a very secure anchor. If you can, put the trailing thread into an area where you'll be doing additional quilting. In this way, the trailing thread can be further secured.

If you're working in a frame or in a hoop on a stand, you'll find that it's easier to quilt in some directions than in others. If I quilt with my fingers on the needle, I find I can quilt at most angles as long as I'm moving generally right to left (I'm right-handed). With rocking quilting, I quilt generally downward, or toward my body. With some patterns, it's tempting to try to quilt around in circles or squares. If you try this method, you'll find yourself going in an awkward direction half of the time.

You'll go faster if you quit only in directions that are comfortable for you. If you must go around a shape, try the trick of starting a thread in the middle and quilting with both ends of the thread.

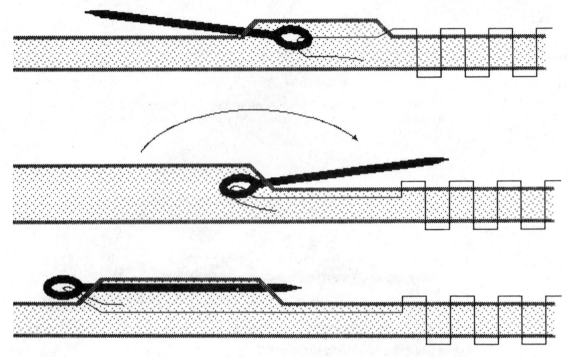

Fig. 4–13. These cross sections show how to end a thread when there is no nearby seam line. The needle is slipped inside the quilt its whole length (top). The needle then is pulled almost all the way through, and turned end over end (middle). Finally, the needle is pushed through the batting, eye first (bottom). By continuing end over end in this manner, you can bury a long tail of thread in the quilt.

Machine Quilting

Machine quilting is one of those skills that takes practice. The first time I tried, I did everything wrong, and was so discouraged that I didn't try again for years. When I was willing to try again, I still had some struggles, but the speed of machine quilting has made it worthwhile.

Machine quilting works best with designs that don't change direction often, since rotating the quilt under the needle can be a big chore with a large and bulky quilt. The quilt must be bundled or rolled up so that it fits under the sewing arm, and rolling and unrolling and rerolling when you change directions can be a major hassle. Designs with continuous lines work better than designs where you must start and stop the thread often. Starts and stops are not particularly difficult in themselves, but every start or stop leaves two dangling threads, one on the back and one on the front, and all those threads have to be hidden. Designs with crossing lines also can be a problem, since little wrinkles and tucks are likely to develop where two lines of stitching cross.

If you're working on a large quilt, the weight of the quilt will need to be supported so that it won't pull on the quilt and work against you as you sew. At the least, you'll need a table to the left of the sewing machine, where it can support most of the weight of the quilt. If you can manage it, set up another table behind the sewing machine.

The main problem with machine quilting is the tendency for the layers to slip. The slippage causes wrinkling, and acute wrinkling can cause little tucks in either the top or the back of the quilt. There are two keys to preventing wrinkling and tucking problems: adequate basting, and a presser foot that creates a minimum of friction. The simplest foot is a *straight-stitch presser foot,* a narrow foot with a hole rather than the slot for the needle to go through. The foot's narrowness will cut down on drag. A *roller foot,* with a roller built into the foot, also can cut down on drag. For me, the answer was a *walking foot,* or *even-feed foot,* which is a complex gadget, bulkier than a regular foot, with parts that attach farther up the shaft. The foot is lifted off the fabric between stitches and so appears to "walk." When, in spite of everything, I still occasionally get tucks, I rip out about 3 inches of quilting and restitch.

Start quilting by setting the stitch length to zero and making three or four stitches to form a kind of knot. Then reset the stitch length to about 3 mm, or 8 stitches to the inch. As you sew, resist the temptation to push the fabric under the presser foot. Instead, pull out from the needle to the sides. Even if slight crossways wrinkles form in front of the needle, they magically disappear in the sewing, and the stitching comes out smooth.

After you have finished all the quilting, there are still all those thread ends to deal with. I pull the thread end on the back of the quilt, trying to pull the front thread through to the back of the quilt so that I can hide front and back threads at the same time. If the front thread won't come easily, I deal with it separately. I use a needle with a big, easily threaded eye and pull the thread ends inside the quilt.

BINDING

There are a number of ways to finish the edge of a quilt, but most people use a binding, which reinforces the edge while finishing it. I use bias binding because I find I can keep it from wrinkling. I'm also fond of the candy-stripe effect you get by cutting bias binding from a striped fabric.

You can purchase wide bias binding in stores, but it's often made from loosely woven, low-quality cloth. I usually cut my own binding, so I can choose the width and fabric for the binding. I usually use 1½-inch bias strips, but I use wider strips for heavier fabrics. For pieces without batting, I use 1-inch bias strips.

In any method for cutting binding, the key is marking the first bias line. Once that line is established, you can mark and cut bias strips in any of the ways you cut straight strips. On scraps, you can mark a bias line by placing a triangle on the grain of the fabric, then marking a 45-degree line. If you're using yardage, it's easier to fold a bias line. Square off the end of the fabric, then fold as shown in Fig. 4–14.

If you're cutting a lot of binding or if you're a little short of fabric, you might want to use the "parallelogram trick" to get the maximum amount of binding from your fabric. Trim the fabric so that you have a rectangle with straight edges and good square corners, then follow the steps shown in Fig. 4–15. Join the bias strips as shown in Fig. 4–16.

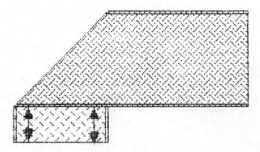

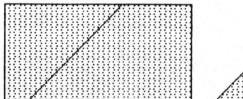

Fig. 4–14. To fold a bias line, fold the end of the fabric over so that it is parallel with the selvage.

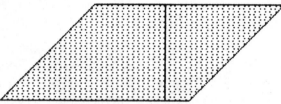

Fig. 4–15. To maximize the amount of bias binding that can be cut from a rectangle, first cut the rectangle along a bias line to form two trapezoids. Switch the positions of the two trapezoids, then sew them together to form a parallelogram, as shown.

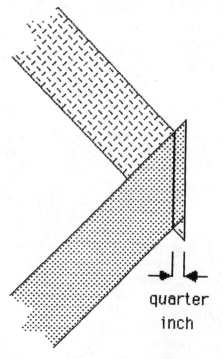

quarter
inch

Fig. 4–16. Two pieces of bias strip are joined as shown. Right sides are placed together, and the pieces are adjusted so that the bias edges cross ¼ inch from the ends of the strips.

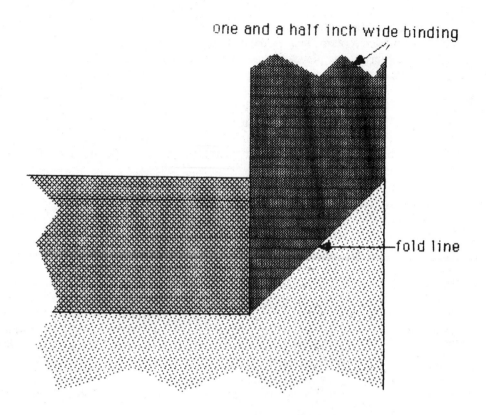

one and a half inch wide binding

fold line

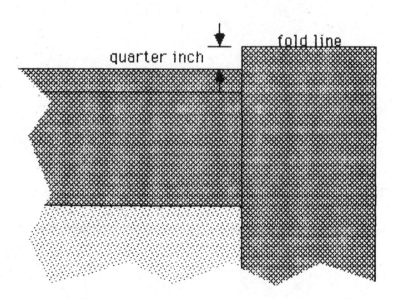

quarter inch

fold line

Fig. 4–17. The first step in folding a bias strip is to go around the corner of a quilt (top). The second fold then is made (bottom). The quarter-inch "extension" shown is the right size for 1½-inch binding.

Before you sew on the binding, check the basting around the edge of the quilt. If there are wrinkled spots, redo it. You will sew the binding by machine to the front side of the quilt. Start at any place except a corner of the quilt, and lay the binding face down on the quilt top, aligning the edge of the binding with the edge of the quilt top. Place the quilt under the sewing machine, with the needle about 1 inch from the end of the binding and a ¼ inch from the edge. Start sewing by backstitching ½ inch, then sew the binding to the quilt with a quarter-inch seam allowance, until you get close to the corner of the quilt. Mark a point on the corner of the quilt ¼ inch in from each edge. Pin the binding to the quilt at this point, sew up to the point, then backstitch away from it.

Fold the binding as shown in Fig. 4–17. Note the ¼ inch between the edge of the quilt and the folded edge of the binding indicated in the diagram. I think of the fold in the bias binding as extending beyond the edge of the quilt. The length of this extension is the difference between the width of the seam allowance (¼ inch) and the finished width of the binding (in this case, ½ inch, since the 1½-inch binding consists of two quarter-inch seam allowances, ½ inch on the front of the quilt, and ½ inch on the back of the quilt). If this extension is too long, there will be too much binding on the corner of the quilt, and the binding will stick out in a point. If this extension is too short, there will not be enough binding, and the corner will be scrunched up. If you were using 1-inch binding, then there would be no extension, since the finished width of the binding would be ¼ inch, the same as the width of the seam allowance. Start the next side by backstitching to the corner point.

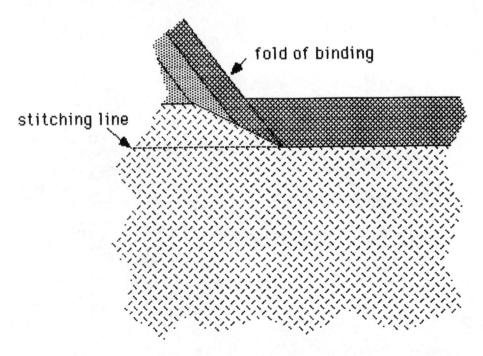

fold of binding

stitching line

Fig. 4 – 18. This close-up of the back side of a quilt shows how the edge of the binding is folded under ¼ inch and the fold is lined up with the stitching line.

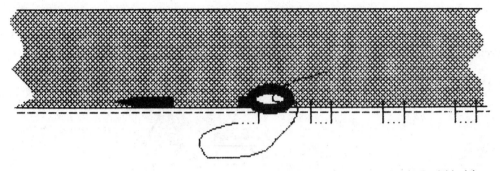

Fig. 4–19. In this view of the back side of the quilt, the needle is taking a stitch inside the fold of the binding. The needle does not penetrate the quilt in this part of the stitch. The dashed line is the back side of the stitching line that holds the binding to the front side of the quilt. The short dotted lines just below this stitching line represent the short stitches into the back of the quilt that hold the binding in place. These short stitches should not come through to the front of the quilt.

When you get back to the place where the binding started, fold the beginning of the binding out of the way. Stitch along the remaining seam allowance, up to the point where the binding began, and then backstitch. By hand, stitch the two ends of the binding together, using either a straight or a slanted seam. A slanted seam usually looks better, especially with a striped binding, but a straight seam might be easier to sew.

Trim the excess batting and backing on the edges of the quilt. If you're using 1½-inch binding, you should trim to ½ inch from the edge of the top, leaving ¾ inch of batting and backing outside the seam. The binding finishes only ½ inch wide, but the extra batting gives fullness to the bound edge. A limp, empty binding looks sort of pitiful.

On the back of the quilt, turn the edge of the binding under ¼ inch and sew it to the back of the quilt by hand, as shown in Fig. 4–18. Sew with a blind stitch, shown in Fig. 4–19.

SIGNING THE QUILT

I usually sign my quilts by stitching my name, the name I've given to the quilt, and the year somewhere in the lower left-hand corner of the quilt top. I use simple straight-stitch lettering that's about ¼ inch tall.

For presentation pieces, I make a more conspicuous embroidered label, which I sew onto the back of the quilt. Figure 4–20 shows an example, which was cross-stitched over waste canvas. I find it easier to do the embroidery on a separate label than directly on the quilt back. I'd also use a label to sign a quilt in ink, since it's less risky than marking on the quilt back. You also can sign and date a quilt in the quilting, and this is the least conspicuous type of signature.

Fig. 4–20. This label was embroidered separately, then attached to the back of a quilt.

Chapter 5
Multiple-Band Patterns

Come-On is made from two kinds of segments sewn together alternately. Many other pieced and repieced patterns also are made by sewing together segments cut from two or more different bands. Rather complex patterns can be made from even just two bands if the widths of the segments are varied. Increasing the number of bands is another way to devise more complex patterns. The ordering of segments from different bands also affects the pattern. If only two kinds of segments are used, segments must be alternated, but with three or more segments, there are many more possibilities for arrangement.

Throughout this chapter are diagrams of design elements that illustrate these various possibilities. Some elements have been used for patterns that have been developed into projects. For each project, there is a construction diagram surrounded with tick marks. The tick marks can be used to draw a grid on top of the construction diagram. Simply connect the tick marks with a colored pencil. Use colored pencil to avoid confusion between the grid lines and the seam lines shown in the diagram.

TWO-SEGMENT PATTERNS

Figure 5–1 shows eight elements and patterns that can be made with two segments. Come-On is made of elements like those in the third and fourth rows of the first column. Figure 5–2 shows how these elements can be varied by using different widths of segments and how shifting from wide A segments to wide B segments can change the pattern.

Summer/Winter Weave

Summer/Winter Weave uses the switching trick illustrated in Fig. 5–2. The pattern breaks up vertically into three sections, with pairs of narrow segments marking the breaks (Fig. 5–3.) Another switching trick creates the horizontal breaks that divide the pattern into five horizontal sections. Together the horizontal and vertical breaks create a sort of checkerboard of light and dark areas in the quilt. The checkerboard effect might not be obvious when you first look at the diagram, but it will appear if you squint at it. The pattern was named after a group of weaving patterns that have similar light and dark areas.

The yardages for borders, backing, and binding given in Table 5–1 are based on a border about 4 inches wide. The border width affects the size of the finished quilt, but is critical only for the backing yardage. If the backing fabric is narrower than the quilt, you will need to piece the backing by sewing together two pieces so that there is one crosswise seam in the middle of the backing. If your quilt is close to 45 inches wide, go ahead and buy enough fabric to piece the backing. Most so-called 45-inch-wide fabric is actually somewhat narrower, and almost certainly will be narrower when you have washed it and removed the selvages.

As shown, the quilt is made of 16 dark and 15 light fabrics. These could be scrap-bag fabrics, but you might want to impose some order on them. In my first Summer/Winter Weave quilt, the colors of both the dark and the light fabrics shaded from purple to blue to green (Fig. C–3). The quilt can also, of course, be made with only two fabrics—one light and one dark.

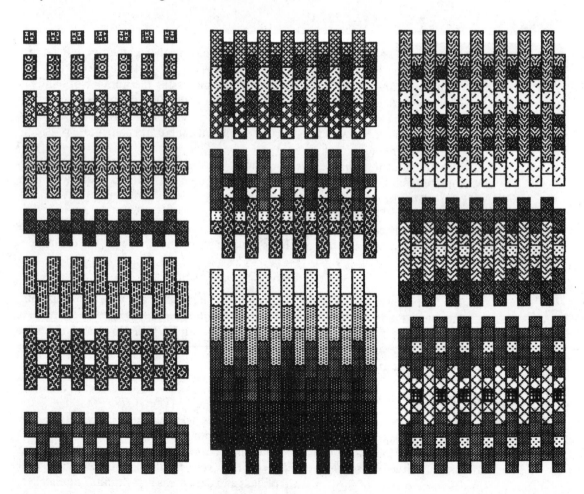

Fig. 5–1. The first column shows simple elements for two-band quilts. The second and third columns show how these elements can be combined to create patterns. The fill patterns used in the combinations are not always the same as those used for the elements.

Table 5 – 1. Strips for Summer/Winter Weave Quilt.

GRID SIZE: **1** ″ Finished Size of Pattern Area: **37** ″ × **61** ″

	BAND A **(27 ″ strips)**	BAND B **(19 1/2 ″ strips)**
Each of 2 dark fabrics (Rows 1, 31)	2 1/2 ″ × 27 ″	1 1/2 ″ × 19 1/2 ″
Each of 6 dark fabrics (Rows 3, 5, 15, 17, 27, 29)	3 1/2 ″ × 27 ″	1 1/2 ″ × 19 1/2 ″
Each of 4 dark fabrics (Rows 9, 11, 21, 23)	1 1/2 ″ × 27 ″	3 1/2 ″ × 19 1/2 ″
Each of 4 dark fabrics (Rows 7, 13, 19, 25)	2 1/2 ″ × 27 ″	2 1/2 ″ × 19 1/2 ″
Each of 9 light fabrics (Rows 2, 4, 6, 14, 16, 18, 26, 28, 30)	1 1/2 ″ × 27 ″	3 1/2 ″ × 19 1/2 ″
Each of 6 light fabrics (Rows 8, 10, 12, 20, 22, 24)	3 1/2 ″ × 27 ″	1 1/2 ″ × 19 1/2 ″

SHOPPING LIST

Pattern: 1/4 yard (or less) of each of 31 fabrics, 16 dark and 15 light.

Border: For seamless borders, 2 yards 45 ″ wide fabric. For pieced borders, about 3/4 yard of 45 ″ wide fabric.

Backing: 2 yards 45 ″ wide fabric.

Batting: About 48 ″ × 72 ″.

Binding: About 6 1/3 yards of 1 1/2 ″ binding. Can be purchased or cut from 1/4 yard of fabric.

Because this quilt has some narrow and some wide segments, you will need to construct special paper templates for marking the cross-cut lines. Band A has three wide segments, then four narrow segments, then three wide segments. Band B has three narrow, then three wide, then three narrow segments. The templates should be marked as follows:

Band A: 3½, 7, 10½, 12, 13½, 15, 16½, 20, 23½, 27
Band B: 1½, 3, 4½, 8, 11½, 15, 16½, 18, 19½

In this quilt, all seam lines fall on the grid. Segments fit together pretty much like those used for Come-On. The distance between a seam in one segment and the next seam in the other segment is always 1 inch.

I quilt this pattern as shown in Fig. 5 – 4. All the vertical quilting lines are unbroken, and each runs down the center of a narrow segment. The horizontal quilting lines that run through the switch rows also are unbroken. The other horizontal quilting lines stop at the vertical breaks. I chose this quilting design because each large, square piece in the pattern is surrounded by quilting, but no quilting cuts through any large square.

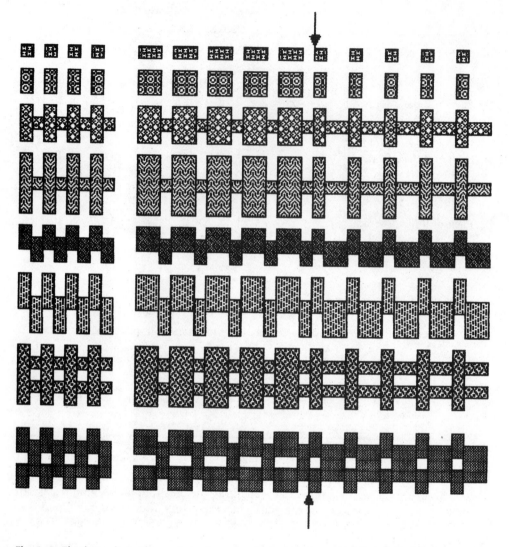

Fig. 5-2. The first column shows elements made of segments that are all the same width. The second column shows how these elements change when one set of segments is wider than the other. To the left of the arrows, segments from one band are shown wider, while to the right of the arrows segments from the other band are shown wider.

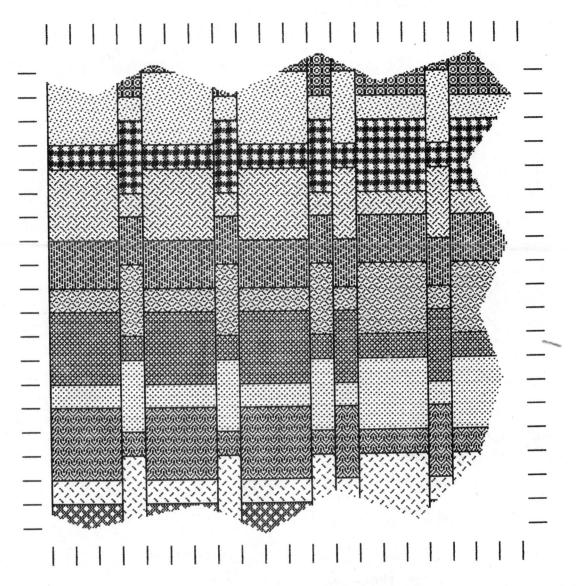

Fig. 5 – 3. This close-up drawing of a corner of the Summer/Winter Weave quilt is surrounded with tick marks. The tick marks can be connected to draw a 1-inch grid, which can be useful as a reference in constructing the quilt.

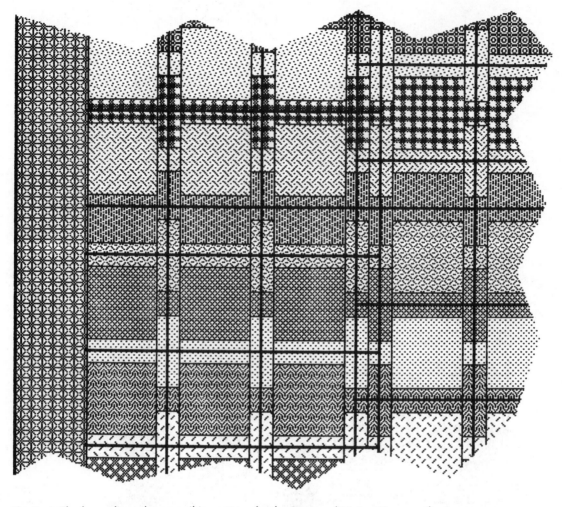

Fig. 5–4. The heavy lines show a quilting pattern for the Summer/Winter Weave quilt.

PATTERNS USING THREE BANDS

At first thought, the logical thing to do with three kinds of segments is to repeat them in a cyclical arrangement: ABC, ABC, etc. However, three-segment motifs which, like those in Fig. 5–5, use the "mirrored" arrangement ABCB,ABCB, etc., turn out to be more useful. The A and C segments are the "mirrors" because, if you start from either an A or a C segment the pattern looks the same in both directions. The pattern repeats every four segments, but the number of segments in a pattern area is usually one more than a multiple of four so that the pattern can start and end with an A segment.

Note that the pattern elements in the third column of Fig. 5–5 have some wide and some narrow segments. None of these has been developed into a project in this book. This is one of the many unexplored areas in pieced and repieced quilting.

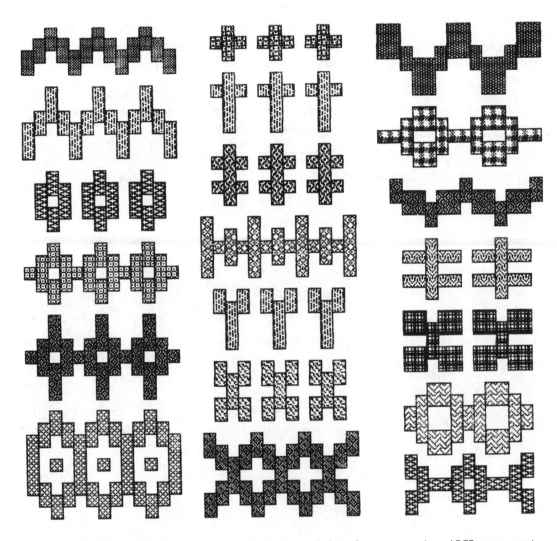

Fig. 5–5. The first two columns show elements that can be made from three segments in an ABCB arrangement. The last column shows variations on some of these elements formed by varying the widths of the segments.

Fused Diamonds

Note that the segments run horizontally on the Fused Diamonds quilt shown in Figs. 5–6 and 5–7. The design elements are like those in the fourth row of the first column of Fig. 5–5. (See Table 5–2.)

For this quilt, you'll need a paper template marked every 2 inches. The distances between seams in adjoining strips are always 1 ½ inches. Unless you use a border more than about 7 inches wide, you will not need to piece the backing.

The quilting pattern shown in Fig. 5–8 runs through the T-joints of the piecing pattern. Each point at which the quilting pattern changes direction is ¾ inch from the top, bottom, and one side of the rectangle.

Table 5–2. Strips for Fused Diamonds Quilt.

GRID SIZE: **1 1/2"** Finished Size of Pattern Area: **37 1/2" × 28 1/2"**

	BAND A (14" strips)	BAND B (24" strips)	BAND C (12" strips)
Fabric 1	1 @ 3 1/2" × 14"	1 @ 3 1/2" × 24"	1 @ 2" × 12"
Fabric 2	1 @ 2" × 14"		
Fabric 3	1 @ 2" × 14"	1 @ 5" × 24"	2 @ 3 1/2" × 12"
Fabric 4			1 @ 2" × 12"
Fabric 5	2 @ 3 1/2" × 14"	1 @ 5" × 24"	1 @ 2" × 12"
Fabric 6	1 @ 2" × 14"		
Fabric 7	1 @ 2" × 14"	1 @ 5" × 24"	2 @ 3 1/2" × 12"
Fabric 8			1 @ 2" × 12"
Fabric 9	2 @ 3 1/2" × 14"	1 @ 5" × 24"	1 @ 2" × 12"
Fabric 10	1 @ 2" × 14"		
Fabric 11	1 @ 2" × 14"	1 @ 5" × 24"	2 @ 3 1/2" × 12"
Fabric 12			1 @ 2" × 12"
Fabric 13	1 @ 3 1/2" × 14"	1 @ 3 1/2" × 24"	1 @ 2" × 12"
Fabric 14	1 @ 2" × 14"		

SHOPPING LIST

Odd-Numbered Fabrics: For each, 1/4 yard 45" wide fabric.

Even-Numbered Fabrics: Scraps 2" × 14".

Backing: 1 3/8 yards 45" wide fabric. For a mitered border, 1 3/8 yards fabric.

Border: For a mitered border, 1 3/8 yards fabric.
For a 4" abutted border, 1/2 yard 45" wide fabric.

Batting: About 43" × 52".

Binding: About 5 yards of 1 1/2" binding. Can be purchased or cut from 1/4 yard of fabric.

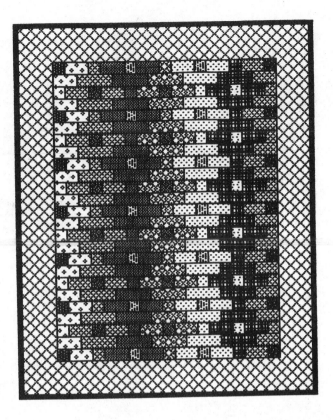

Fig. 5–6. The pattern area for this completed Fused Diamonds quilt is made of segments from three bands in an ABCB arrangement.

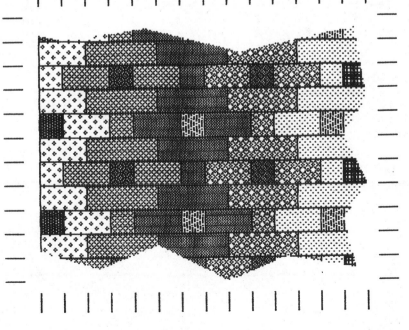

Fig. 5–7. This construction drawing for the Fused Diamonds quilt includes tick marks for drawing a 1½-inch grid.

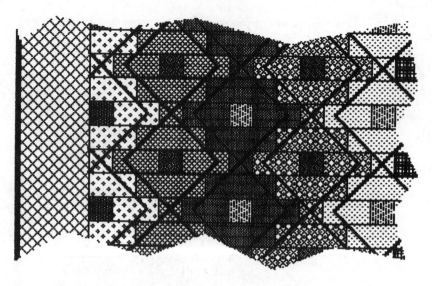

Fig. 5–8. The heavy lines show a quilted pattern for the Fused Diamonds quilt.

Table 5–3. Strips for Eva's Diamonds Place Mats, Set of Eight.

GRID SIZE: **1/2″** Finished Size of Pattern Area: **11″ × 17″**

	BAND A **(60″ strips)**	BAND B **(72″ strips)**	BAND C **(48″ strips)**
Fabric 1	2 @ 3″ × 60″	2 @ 2″ × 72″	2 @ 1″ × 48″
Fabric 2	2 @ 2 1/2″ × 60″	2 @ 2 1/2″ × 72″	2 @ 2 1/2″ × 48″
Fabric 3	1 @ 2 1/2″ × 60″	2 @ 2″ × 72″	2 @ 2″ × 48″
Fabric 4		1 @ 1 1/2″ × 72″	1 @ 3 1/2″ × 48″

SHOPPING LIST
- Fabric 1: 5/8 yard 45″ wide fabric.
- Fabric 2: 7/8 yard 45″ wide fabric.
- Fabric 3: 5/8 yard 45″ wide fabric.
- Fabric 4: 3/8 yard 45″ wide fabric.
- Border: 5/8 yard 45″ wide fabric.
- Backing: 1 3/4 yard 45″ wide fabric.
- Batting: Optional.
  For the ''pillow'' method, 8 pieces each 13 1/2″ × 19 1/2″.
  For the ''quilt'' method, 8 pieces each 15″ × 21″.
- Binding: Optional. If used, about 14 1/4 yards 1″ wide binding. Can be purchased or cut from 3/8 yard 45″ wide fabric.

Eva's Diamonds

The Eva's Diamonds pattern (Figs. 5–9 and C–4) is related to the Fused Diamonds design, but each diamond has a plus sign in the center, rather than a single square. The strips for these place mats are all longer than 45 inches, so you will need to cut them in more than one piece. (See Table 5–3.) As for the Come-On place mats, it might be easier to cut twice as many strips, each half as long. In effect, you'd be making two sets of four place mats. You'll need a paper template marked every 1½ inches.

Some of the seam lines are halfway between grid lines, and in fact the top of the pattern area is halfway between tick marks. Where rectangles of the same fabric meet,

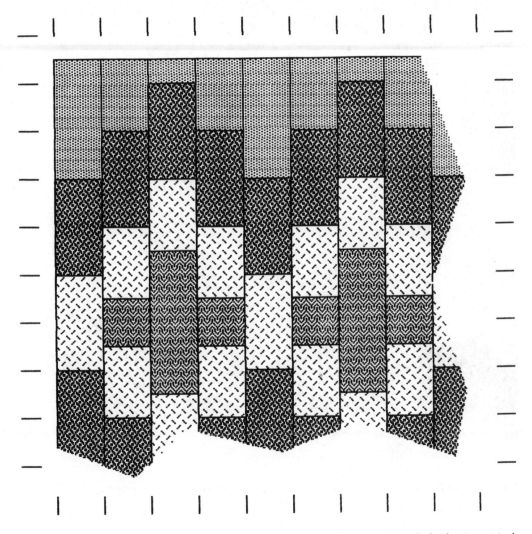

Fig. 5–9. The construction drawing for the Eva's Diamonds place mats includes tick marks for drawing a 1-inch grid.

they usually overlap by 1 inch, but the overlap between rectangles of the lightest fabric are only ½ inch. With overlaps this small, it's important to measure and pin fairly carefully as you sew the segments together.

In the quilting pattern shown in Fig. 5 – 10, the stitching is about 1/16 inch from the seam lines, but you also could quilt this pattern in the ditch. A pattern with this many turns is slow to quilt by machine. It would be very slow with a large quilt that had to be heaved around at every turn, but it's manageable with a small project like these place mats.

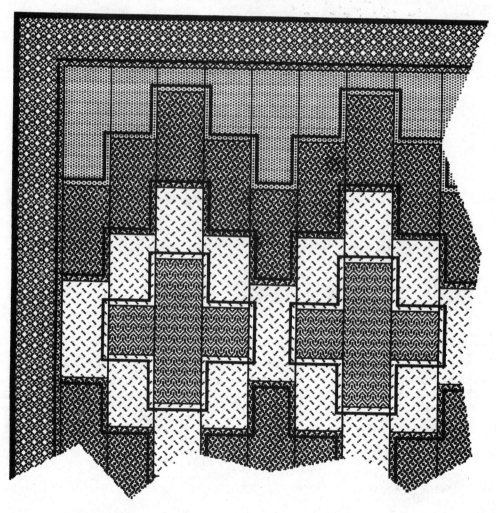

Fig. 5 – 10. The heavy lines show a quilting pattern for the Eva's Diamond place mats.

Striped Sampler

Figures 5–11 and C–5 show the Striped Sampler quilt, named for the variety of ABCBA elements it contains (Fig. 5–12). This quilt is a natural for a scrap quilt, since no more than ¼ yard is needed for any fabric in the pattern area.

The many different fabrics in the pattern area might make the choice of a border fabric difficult. If the border is too much like any of the fabrics in the pattern area, the two fabrics might run together visually. In this quilt, the pattern area and the main border have been separated with a dark, narrow border. A narrow border like this can be considerably darker than any of the fabrics in the pattern area, and thus definitely distinct from all of them, without overwhelming the quilt the way a dark, wide border would. When I use this kind of narrow inner border, I often use the same fabric for the binding.

The yardages in Table 5–4 are based on 10-inch borders since four 10-inch border pieces will fit side by side on 45-inch-wide fabric. For a wider border, you'd need to find wider border fabric or double the yardage. I probably would use the 10-inch border, rather than trying to make a quilt large enough so that, like a bedspread, it would fall to the floor and have extra fabric for folding under the pillows. A bedspread for even a twin bed can be 5½ × 8 feet—a tremendous area. One way to use a smaller quilt on a bed is to put it on top of a plain bedspread in a coordinating color.

You could quilt the Striped Sampler quilt in the ditch like the machine-quilted Come-On, or you could make it a sampler of quilting patterns as well as of piecing patterns. Some quilting suggestions are shown in Fig. 5–13. The quilting follows the fabrics, so the quilting thread could be color-coordinated with the fabrics. All the ends and turning points of the quilting fall on the grid or halfway between points on the grid.

PATTERNS FROM FOUR OR MORE BANDS

With larger numbers of segment types, patterns naturally can become more complex. Some four-segment mirrored elements are shown in Fig. 5–14, and some five-segment mirrored elements in Fig. 5–15.

The practical limit to the number of types of segments you can use in a pattern is the number of repeats you can get into your quilt. A four-segment, mirrored pattern repeats in six segments; a five-segment, mirrored pattern in eight segments; and so on. If you make a quilt with a small number of segments in each of a large number of bands, then the piecing-and-repiecing technique is not saving you much work.

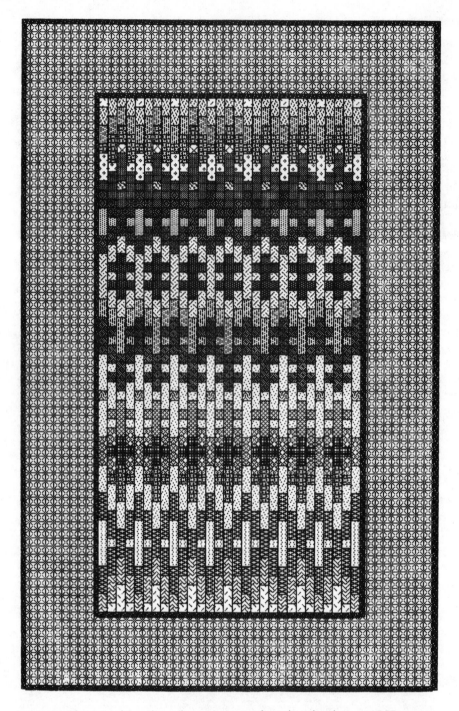

Fig. 5–11. The Striped Sampler quilt uses segments from three bands in an ABCB arrangement. A variety of elements are combined to create the sampler effect.

Table 5–4. Strips for Striped Sampler Quilt.

GRID SIZE: **1**″ Finished Size of Pattern Area: **29**″ × **56**″

	BAND A (12″ strips)	BAND B (21″ strips)	BAND C (10 1/2″ strips)
Fabric 1 (square)	1 @ 1 1/2″ × 12″		
Fabric 2	1 @ 2 1/2″ × 12″	1 @ 2 1/2″ × 21″	1 @ 1 1/2″ × 10 1/2″
Fabric 3	1 @ 2 1/2″ × 12″	1 @ 2 1/2″ × 21″	1 @ 2 1/2″ × 10 1/2″
Fabric 4	1 @ 1 1/2″ × 12″	1 @ 3 1/2″ × 21″	1 @ 2 1/2″ × 10 1/2″
Fabric 5 (square)			1 @ 1 1/2″ × 10 1/2″
Fabric 6 (plus)	1 @ 3 1/2″ × 12″	1 @ 1 1/2″ × 21″	
Fabric 7	1 @ 1 1/2″ × 12″	1 @ 3 1/2″ × 21″	1 @ 3 1/2″ × 10 1/2″
			1 @ 2 1/2″ × 10 1/2″
Fabric 8 (square)			1 @ 1 1/2″ × 10 1/2″
Fabric 9	2 @ 2 1/2″ × 12″	2 @ 2 1/2″ × 21″	1 @ 3 1/2″ × 10 1/2″
Fabric 10 (plus)	1 @ 3 1/2″ × 12″	1 @ 1 1/2″ × 21″	
Fabric 11	1 @ 5 1/2″ × 12″	2 @ 2 1/2″ × 21″	2 @ 2 1/2″ × 10 1/2″
		1 @ 1 1/2″ × 21″	
Fabric 12		2 @ 1 1/2″ × 21″	1 @ 5 1/2″ × 10 1/2″
Fabric 13	1 @ 2 1/2″ × 12″	1 @ 2 1/2″ × 21″	1 @ 4 1/2″ × 10 1/2″
		1 @ 1 1/2″ × 21″	
Fabric 14	1 @ 4 1/2″ × 12″	2 @ 1 1/2″ × 21″	1 @ 4 1/2″ × 10 1/2″
		1 @ 2 1/2″ × 21″	
Fabric 15	2 @ 4 1/2″ × 12″	2 @ 1 1/2″ × 21″	1 @ 1 1/2″ × 10 1/2″
		1 @ 3 1/2″ × 21″	
Fabric 16 (square)	1 @ 1 1/2″ × 12″		
Fabric 17 (cross)		1 @ 1 1/2″ × 21″	1 @ 4 1/2″ × 10 1/2″
Fabric 18	1 @ 3 1/2″ × 12″	2 @ 2 1/2″ × 21″	
Fabric 19 (plus)		1 @ 1 1/2″ × 21″	1 @ 3 1/2″ × 10 1/2″
Fabric 20 (cross)		1 @ 1 1/2″ × 21″	1 @ 4 1/2″ × 10 1/2″
Fabric 21	1 @ 3 1/2″ × 12″	1 @ 3 1/2″ × 21″	1 @ 3 1/2″ × 10 1/2″
Fabric 22	2 @ 3 1/2″ × 12″	2 @ 3 1/2″ × 21″	1 @ 3 1/2″ × 10 1/2″
Fabric 23	1 @ 5 1/2″ × 12″	1 @ 1 1/2″ × 21″	
Fabric 24	1 @ 2 1/2″ × 12″	1 @ 3 1/2″ × 21″	1 @ 3 1/2″ × 10 1/2″
Fabric 25		1 @ 1 1/2″ × 21″	1 @ 3 1/2″ × 10 1/2″

SHOPPING LIST

Fabrics: Scraps, no more than 1/4 yard for each

Inner Border: 1/4 yard 45″ wide fabric.

Border: For a mitered border, 2 1/4 yards 45″ wide fabric. For an abutted border, 1 5/8 yards 45″ wide fabric.

Backing: For fabric wider than the quilt, 2 yards.
For fabric narrower than the quilt, 3 yards.

Batting: About 54″ × 81″.

Binding: About 7 yards 1 1/2″ wide binding. Can be purchased, or cut from 3/8 yard of 45″ fabric. If narrow border and binding are made from same fabric, 1/2 yard is sufficient for both.

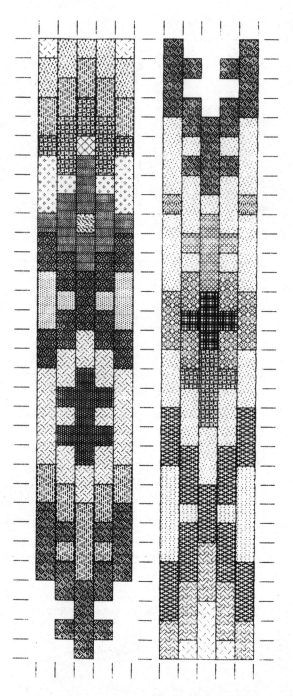

Fig. 5 – 12. This construction drawing for the Striped Sampler has been divided into two sections. The last part of the pattern in the left-hand section is repeated at the top of the right-hand section. The tick marks can be used for drawing a 1-inch grid.

Fig. 5 – 13. The heavy lines show a quilting pattern for the Striped Sampler quilt.

Fig. 5–14. Both columns show elements composed of four segments in a mirrored (ABCDCB) arrangement.

Fig. 5–15. Both columns show elements composed of five segments in a mirrored (ABCDEDCB) arrangment.

Christmas Trees

The Christmas Trees pattern, with the trees arranged top to top, was designed for a tablecloth, so that the trees seem to grow from the edges of the table. The pattern has 8 types of segments in a mirrored arrangement, so it repeats in 14 segments.

As shown in Fig. 5–16, the background for the Christmas Trees is white. If you do use plain white fabric, make sure that it is opaque so seam allowances and stray threads don't show through to the front. Light solids tend to be transparent, particularly if the fabric has a high synthetic content. Yardages are based on a 10-inch border, and assume that the backing will be pieced. (See Table 5–5.)

As Fig. 5–17 shows, many of the seams in this pattern fall halfway between grid lines. You'll need a paper template marked every 1½ inches. There are a few very wide strips in the pattern. Rather than making a very wide paper template, you might want to mark the cross-cut lines directly. The kind of cutting guide used with a rotary cutter would be useful for marking the cross-cut lines on these strips.

To finish the tablecloth, pin top and backing right sides together. Sew around the edges, leaving a space for turning. Turn the cloth right side out, then baste the turning space closed. Topstitch around the edge. Smooth the cloth and backing flat, then baste near the edge of the pattern area. Stitch in the ditch all around the pattern area.

Table 5–6 has information for a table runner based on seven repeats of the Christmas Trees pattern. For this project, the grid has been reduced to ½ inch. Follow Fig. 5–16, but keep the reduced grid size in mind. For the runner, the smallest overlaps between adjacent rectangles are only ¼ inch, so you must pin segments together before you sew them.

I do not put batting into a table runner. Instead, I stiffen and stabilize the patchwork top by ironing fusible interfacing to the wrong side. This is an irreversible step, of course, so press the top carefully and be sure that it hasn't been pulled out of square. Cut out a backing the same size as the top, then finish as for the tablecloth.

Ragtime

There are only 4 segments in the Ragtime pattern (Fig. 5–18), but their arrangement is more complicated than the mirrored arrangement used for other patterns in this section. The pattern repeats in 12 segments: ABC,BCD,CDA,DAB. This two-steps-forward-one-step-backward arrangement suggested syncopation to me, and thus the Ragtime name. The arrangement also can be seen as being composed of triples: ABA,BCB,CDC, DAD. The quilt shown includes 2½ repeats on either side of the centerline.

In spite of the pattern's complicated look, all construction lines fall on the grid. The only off-grid lines are at the top and bottom of the quilt, where the pattern is cut off at its turning point. Like the Striped Sampler, Ragtime is shown with ½-inch-wide inner border. You might want to use the same fabric for both the inner border and the binding. The yardages are based on a quilt with a 10-inch-wide outer border. (See Table 5–7.) If you use a 45-inch-wide fabric for the backing, you will need to piece the backing with one seam running lengthwise up the center.

Fig. 5 – 16. The Christmas Trees pattern is shown here as it would appear on a tablecloth. The borders for a tablecloth would probably be much wider than those shown here.

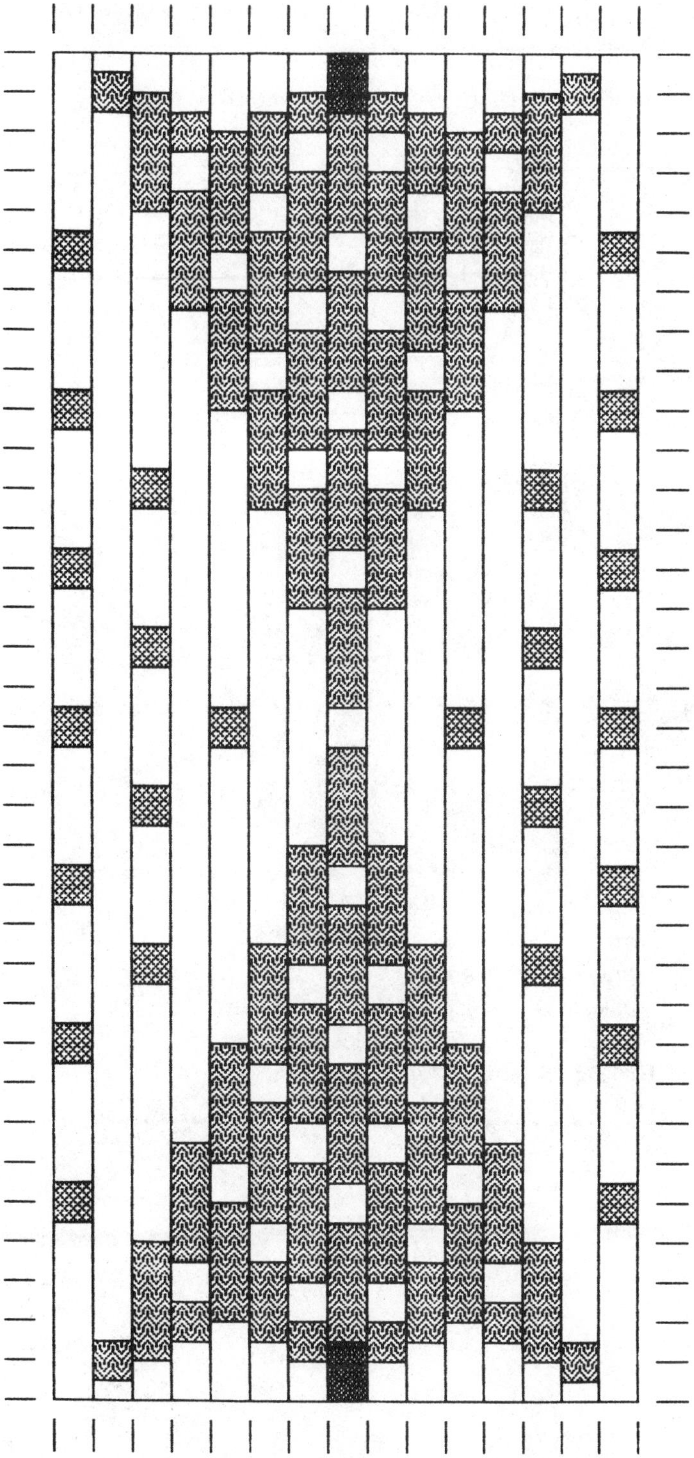

Fig. 5–17. This construction drawing for the Christmas Trees pattern includes tick marks for drawing a grid. For the tablecloth, this is a 1-inch grid, while for the runner it is a ½-inch grid. An assortment of bright colors would be used for the squares on the trees, shown here in white.

Table 5 – 5. Strips for Christmas Tress Tablecloth.

GRID SIZE: **1**″ Finished Size of Pattern Area: **34**″ × **59**″

Fabric 1: Edges   2 @ 34 1/2″ × 1 1/2″
           Band A 2 @ 5″ × 7 1/2″   6 @ 3 1/2″ × 7 1/2″
           Band B 2 @ 1″ × 12″   1 @ 31 1/2″ × 12″
           Band C 2 @ 1 1/2″ × 12″   2 @ 7″ × 12″   3 @ 3 1/2″ × 12″
           Band D 1 @ 21 1/2″ × 12″   1 @ 20 1/2″ × 12″
           Band E 2 @ 2 1/2″ × 12″   2 @ 8″ × 12″
           Band F 2 @ 2″ × 12″   1 @ 11 1/2″ × 12″
           Band G 2 @ 1 1/2″ × 12″   1 @ 6 1/2″ × 12″
           Band H 1 @ 1 1/2″ × 6″

Fabric 2: Band A 7 @ 1 1/2″ × 7 1/2″
           Band C 4 @ 1 1/2″ × 12″
           Band E 1 @ 1 1/2″ × 12″

Fabric 3: Band B 2 @ 1 1/2″ × 12″
           Band C 2 @ 3 1/2″ × 12″
           Band D 2 @ 1 1/2″ × 12″   2 @ 3 1/2″ × 12″
           Band E 4 @ 3 1/2″ × 12″
           Band F 2 @ 2 1/2″ × 12″   4 @ 3 1/2″ × 12″
           Band G 2 @ 1 1/2″ × 12″   6 @ 3 1/2″ × 12″
           Band H 8 @ 3 1/2″ × 6″

Fabric 4: Band H 2 @ 2″ × 6″

7 other fabrics   2 @ 1 1/2″ × 12″

3 other fabrics   2 @ 1 1/2″ × 6″

SHOPPING LIST
  Fabric 1: Background. 1 3/8 yards 45″ wide fabric.
  Fabric 2: Stars. 1/4 yard 45″ wide fabric.
  Fabric 3: Trees. 7/8 yard 45″ wide fabric.
  Fabric 4: Tree trunks. Scrap.
    Others: Decorations on the trees. Scraps.
    Border: 1 7/8 yards 45″ wide fabric.
  Backing: 3 yards 45″ wide fabric.

Table 5 – 6. Strips for Christmas Trees Runner.

GRID SIZE: **1 1/2"** Finished Size of Pattern Area: **17" × 50 1/2"**

Fabric 1:	Edges	2 @ 17 1/2" × 1"		
	Band A	2 @ 2.75" × 8"	6 @ 2" × 8"	
	Band B	2 @ 0.75" × 14"	1 @ 16" × 14"	
	Band C	2 @ 1" × 14"	2 @ 3.75" × 14"	3 @ 2" × 14"
	Band D	1 @ 11" × 14"	1 @ 10 1/2" × 14"	
	Band E	2 @ 1 1/2" × 14"	2 @ 4.25" × 14"	
	Band F	2 @ 1.25" × 14"	1 @ 6" × 14"	
	Band G	2 @ 1" × 14"	1 @ 3 1/2" × 14"	
	Band H	1 @ 1" × 7"		
Fabric 2:	Band A	7 @ 1" × 8"		
	Band C	4 @ 1" × 14"		
	Band E	1 @ 1" × 14"		
Fabric 3:	Band B	2 @ 1" × 14"		
	Band C	2 @ 2" × 14"		
	Band D	2 @ 1" × 14"	2 @ 2" × 14"	
	Band E	4 @ 2" × 14"		
	Band F	2 @ 1 1/2" × 14"	4 @ 2" × 14"	
	Band G	2 @ 1" × 14"	6 @ 2" × 14"	
	Band H	8 @ 2" × 7"		
Fabric 4:	Band H	2 @ 1.25" × 7"		
7 other fabrics		2 @ 1" × 14"		
3 other fabrics		2 @ 1" × 7"		

SHOPPING LIST

Fabric 1: Background. 7/8 yards 45" wide fabric.

Fabric 2: Stars. 1/8 yard 45" wide fabric.

Fabric 3: Trees. 5/8 yard 45" wide fabric.

Fabric 4: Tree trunks. Scrap.

Others: Decorations on the trees. Scraps.

Border: For seamless borders, 1 1/2 yards 45" wide fabric.
For pieced borders, about 3/8 yard 45" wide fabric.

Backing: 1 1/2 yards 45" wide fabric.

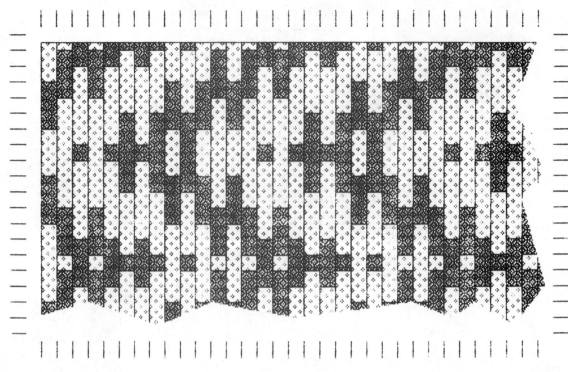

Fig. 5–18. The construction drawing for the Ragtime quilt includes tick marks for drawing a 1-inch grid.

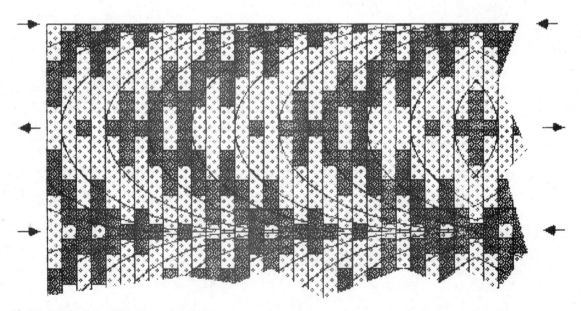

Fig. 5–19. The heavy lines show a quilting pattern for the Ragtime quilt. All the lines are drawn with one template.

Table 5–7. Strips for Ragtime Quilt.

GRID SIZE: **1"** Finished Size of Pattern Area: **59" × 70"**

	BAND A (**21" strips**)	BAND B (**24" strips**)	BAND C (**24" strips**)	BAND D (**19 1/2" strips**)
Fabric 1 (dark)	10 @ 3 1/2" × 21"	10 @ 3 1/2" × 24"	2 @ 2" × 24" 5 @ 1 1/2" × 24" 4 @ 3 1/2" × 24"	2 @ 1" × 19 1/2" 5 @ 5 1/2" × 19 1/2" 4 @ 1 1/2" × 19 1/2"
Fabric 2 (light)	2 @ 3" × 21" 5 @ 3 1/2" × 21" 4 @ 5 1/2" × 21"	2 @ 1" × 24" 5 @ 7 1/2" × 24" 4 @ 1 1/2" × 24"	10 @ 5 1/2" × 24"	10 @ 4 1/2" × 19 1/2"

SHOPPING LIST

Fabric 1: 2 yards 45" wide fabric.
Fabric 2: 3 yards 45" wide fabric.
Inner Border: 1/4 yard 45" wide fabric.
Border: For 10" mitered borders, 2 3/8 yards 45" wide fabric.
For 10" a butted borders, 2 1/8 yards 45" wide fabric.
Backing: 5 1/4 yards 45" wide fabric.
Batting: About 84" × 95".
Binding: About 9 1/2 yards of 1 1/2" binding. Can be purchased or cut from 3/8 yards fabric. If narrow border and binding are made from same fabric, 5/8 yard is sufficient for both.

85

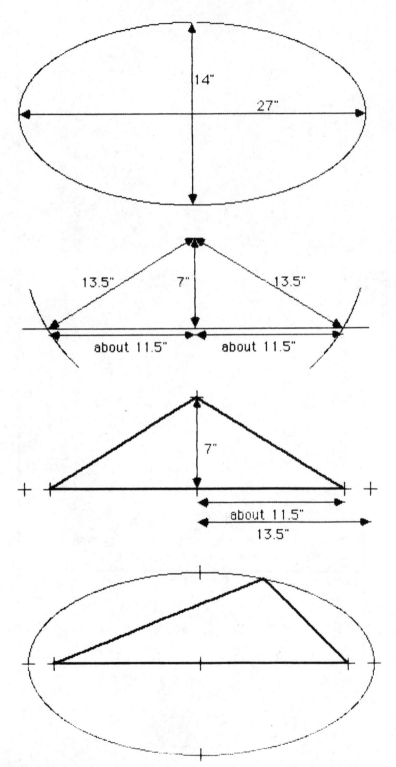

Fig. 5–20. The top drawing shows the ellipse used to quilt the Ragtime quilt. The second drawing shows how to use a compass to find the foci of the ellipse. The heavy line in the third drawing represents a string stretched around tacks placed at the foci and a pencil placed at the top of the ellipse. The bottom drawing shows how the pencil forms an ellipse as it is moved around within the stretched string.

Figure 5 – 19 shows a quilting design for the quilt. A curved quilting line like this is not difficult to sew, but you do need to construct a template for marking it. All the curved lines shown are marked with one template.

Figure 5 – 20 shows the steps for drafting the quilting template. The only tricky part of the process is using tacks and a piece of string to draw the ellipse. Put your drawing on top of a piece of corrugated cardboard, or something into which you can stick tacks. Stick the tacks through the drawing at the foci, and at the top of the ellipse. Tie a string in a triangle around these three tacks, a shown in the third stage of the diagram. Take out the tack at the top of the ellipse, but leave the string looped around the other two tacks. Put a pencil in the loop and, keeping the string taut, move the pencil around in a circular motion. What results is not a circle, but the desired ellipse. If the line you draw is a little jerky, go around more than once, then use a broad-tipped marker to draw a smoothed-out version of the curve.

On the right half of the ellipse, draw vertical lines 1 inch apart, starting with the vertical centerline. You will use these lines as guides for placing the template on the quilt top. Cut this half ellipse out, and cut it into two quarters along the horizontal center line. Glue one quarter-ellipse to a piece of lightweight cardboard, like that used for cereal boxes or tablet backs, using a glue stick or rubber cement. Avoid white glue, which would make the paper wrinkle. Cut out the cardboard.

The template as it stands is the correct shape and has vertical guidelines on one side. Because the template will be used on both sides, it needs guidelines on the other side as well. To supply them, glue the other quarter-ellipse to the other side of the template.

Follow Fig. 5 – 19 for placing the template on the quilt. Note that the pieced pattern can be divided up with imaginary horizontal mirror lines. One kind of mirror line is marked on Fig. 5 – 19 with inward-pointing arrows. The other type of mirror line is marked with outward-pointing arrows. The template has a short edge, a long edge, and a curved edge. The curve is sharper at one end of the curved edge, and shallower at the other end. Place the more sharply curved end of the curved edge on a seam line. Place the long edge of the template on one of the outward-arrow mirror lines. The short edge of the template lines up with the center of a segment. Mark partial ellipses at the outer edge of the quilt. The eye shapes at the center of the quilt also are composed of partial ellipses. Fig. C – 10 shows a completed Ragtime quilt.

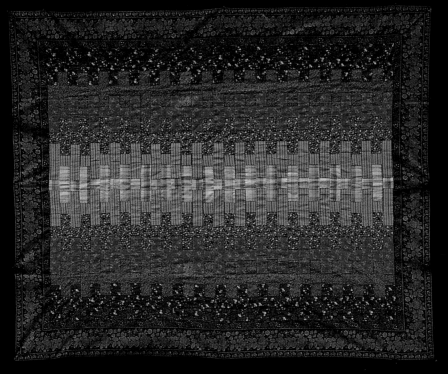

C-2. One of many Come-On variations.

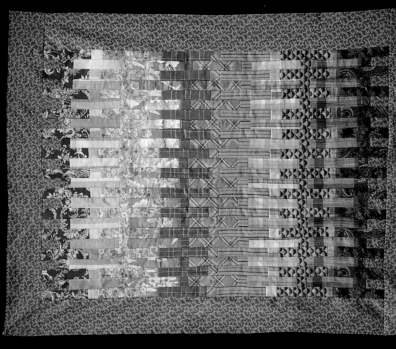

C-1. A Come-On quilt.

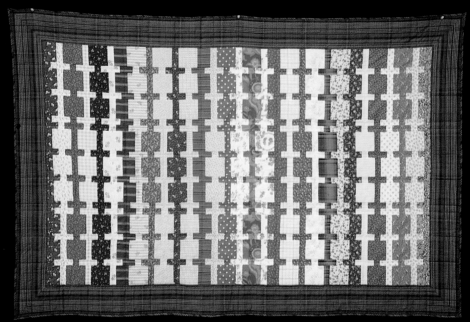

C-3. Summer/Winter Weave.

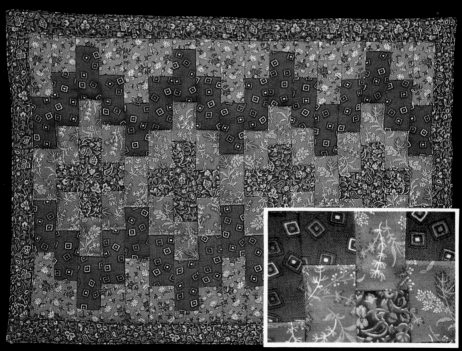

C-4. Eva's Diamonds quilt, with detail.

C-5. Striped Sampler.

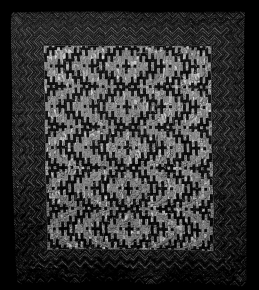

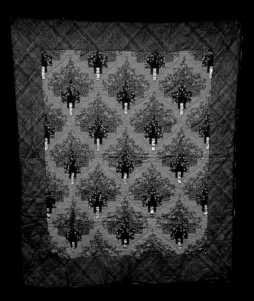

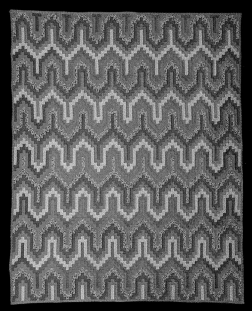

(opposite)

C-6. **Red Wave** (top left).
C-7. **Gentle Rainbow** (top right).
C-8. **Blue Wave** (bottom left).
C-9. **Center Diamond** (bottom right).

(above)

C-10. **Ragtime** (top left).
C-11. **The Vaults** (top right).
C-12. **Peacock Eyes** (bottom left).
C-13. **Standing Wave** (bottom right).

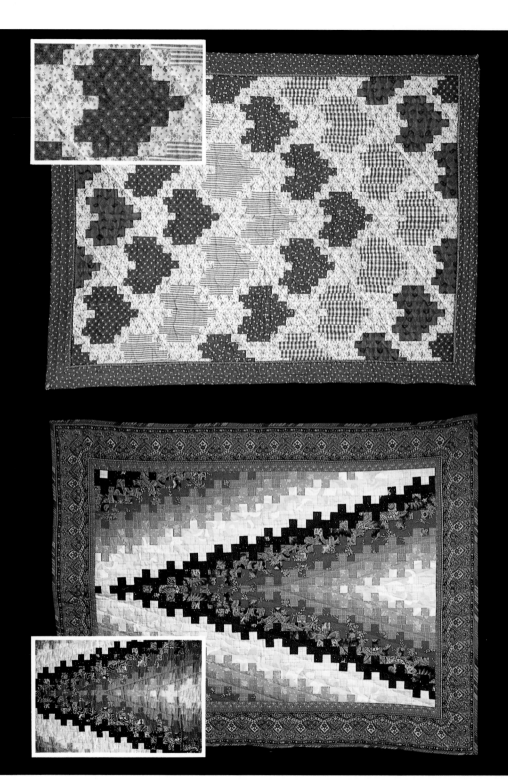

C-15. Heart Throb, with detail.

C-14. Flame Dart, with detail.

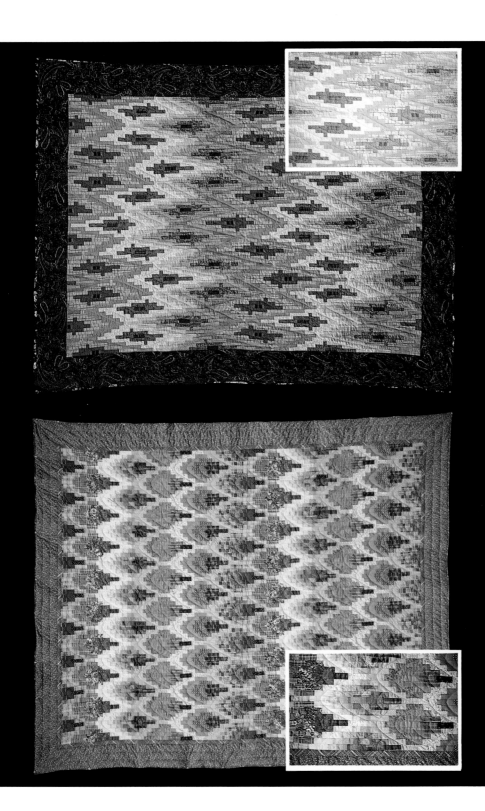

C-17. Spring Tender, with detail.

C-16. Autumn Orchard, with detail.

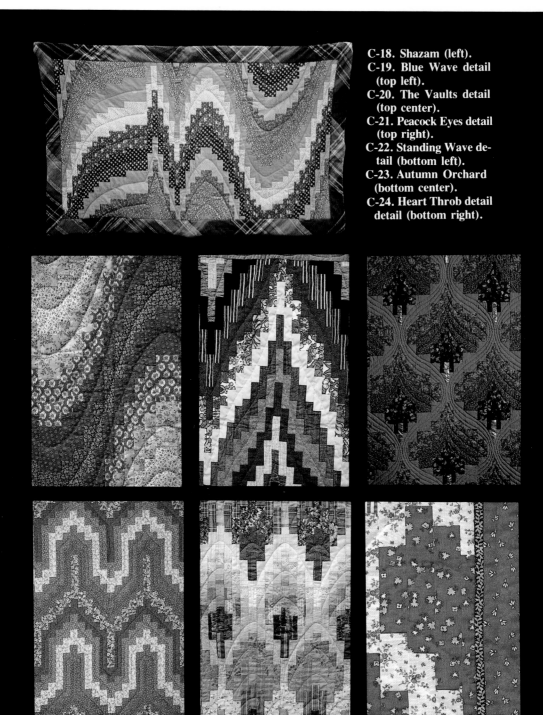

C-18. Shazam (left).
C-19. Blue Wave detail (top left).
C-20. The Vaults detail (top center).
C-21. Peacock Eyes detail (top right).
C-22. Standing Wave detail (bottom left).
C-23. Autumn Orchard (bottom center).
C-24. Heart Throb detail detail (bottom right).

Chapter 6

Choosing
Fabrics
and Colors

Choosing fabrics involves considering several aspects, including physical characteristics, color, and pattern. The choices can be bewildering, and I'm sure you sometimes wish for a few simple rules that would solve all problems. In fact, there are some rules, but none provides absolute answers. Instead, each quilter, as she works, develops a personal style and color sense.

PHYSICAL CHARACTERISTICS OF FABRIC

I use primarily cotton and cotton blends for my quilts. Some quilters use only 100% cotton, but I don't see any good reason to limit myself in this way. For hand appliqué, I would agree that 100% cotton is the fabric of choice, but for machine piecing I don't think it's necessary. When I do reject fabrics, it is usually on the basis of their weight or feel.

The one fiber I never use is *acetate,* a silky synthetic with colors that tend to fade. I expect all the colors in my quilts to change somewhat with time, but acetates commonly fade dramatically in a relatively short time, and I don't want to take chances with them. You can test a fabric for acetate content easily, since it dissolves in nail-polish remover.

For most quilts, I use woven fabrics of a weight that would be used for shirts, blouses, or dresses. Knit fabrics are usually stretchy, requiring different sewing techniques, and many knits are also heavier than I like. Fabrics that are much lighter or much heavier than dress-weight can lead to wear, since a lighter fabric wears out faster when sewn to a heavier fabric. If you're making a quilt to hang on the wall, you can be freer in mixing fabrics. The Vaults, shown in Fig. C–11 and C–20, is such a wall quilt. It contains wool, velvet, corduroy, and a shiny synthetic, as well as more traditional quilting fabrics.

Fabrics that are generally too light include thin, silklike fabrics and anything that's transparent. Thin, silky fabrics are often very limp and hard to work with. Transparent fabrics are a problem because the seam allowances show through. If a thin transparent fabric is otherwise ideal for a quilt you're making, you can use it if you line it. Choose a lightweight solid fabric, probably a white one, as the lining. Cut strips of both the face fabric and the lining fabric and place the lining behind the face fabric. Treat the two layers of fabric as though they were one heavier fabric. You might want to baste them together to prevent slipping.

Fabrics that are too heavy include corduroy, sailcloth, denim, gabardine, and, in general, fabrics that would be used for pants or skirts, rather than dresses or blouses. I sometimes make an entire quilt in these somewhat heavier fabrics, but I usually don't mix them with lighter fabrics. If you make a quilt in heavier fabrics, you might want to use a wider seam allowance, since some of these fabrics will be more coarsely woven, and thus more likely to fray.

I also avoid fabrics that are either too tightly or too loosely woven. Sheeting, especially percale, is so tightly woven that it's hard to get a needle through, which is especially undesirable if you will be quilting by hand. Bargain-table fabrics sometimes can be too loosely woven. If a fabric feels sleazy and if the threads are loosely spaced, if might not be a bargain. Sometimes cheap fabrics have been heavily starched or sized. I avoid really stiff fabrics because, although some will wash up nicely, others will stay stiff, and still others become very limp indeed.

COLOR

Color is an area of insecurity for many quilters, but trying to read up on color in art books can be discouraging, since most discussions of color are based on paint, and talk in terms of mixing pigments. The quilter won't be mixing pigments at all, unless she starts dying her fabrics. Usually she must work with colors that come to her already "mixed." If she decided ahead of time to use a particular color, she probably wouldn't be able to find any fabric in just that shade in the fabric store.

The positive side of this dilemma is that she will find fabrics in colors and combinations of colors that she might never invent by herself. Using colors and patterns that already exist makes her job more complicated than that of a painter who can mix a color to order; however, these same colors and patterns are also a more exciting palette than plain paint.

Characteristics of Color

The most obvious characteristic of a color is its *hue*. That is, is it red, orange, yellow, green, blue, or purple? Or is it some color in between, or a neutral like white, gray, black, or brown? For solid fabrics, this is usually a simple question to answer. For printed fabrics, the answer might not be simple at all. Try arranging your fabrics in rainbow or color-wheel order: red, orange, yellow, green, blue, purple.

When you come to a fabric that's a mixture of colors, back off or squint and look at it again. With distance, the color in the fabric probably will appear to blend, and you'll be better able to assign the fabric a place. In some multicolored fabrics, one color dominates, and will determine the place of the fabric as a whole. In others, the colors seem to "mix" in the way that pigments mix. For instance, most yellow calicos have bits of black and green in the print, and from a distance the fabric has the dirty yellow-green color you'd get by adding a bit of green or black to yellow paint. A few fabrics are persistently multicolored, especially if they're large in scale. A fabric with broad red and white stripes won't look pink unless you move a great distance away from it.

The next most obvious characteristic of color is *value,* its lightness or darkness. Take all your fabrics of one hue and sort them from light to dark. Again, patterned fabrics might cause difficulties. To sort out the values of several fabrics, squint at them or take them to a dim place like a closet. With less light, the hue of the fabric becomes less obvious, and the value more evident. Another trick is to look at the fabrics through red cellophane or clear red plastic, which also wipes out hue. Fabrics with distinct areas of very light and very dark hue will be the most difficult to place in your gradation.

After hue and value, other terms referring to color are less obvious and less universally accepted. Many were developed by painters, and depend on ideas about mixing paints. I find that a third useful term is *clarity*. A color is clear if it looks like one of the crayons in an eight-crayon box: it is bright and simple. Clarity is perhaps best understood in terms of its opposites. Colors that are not clear include those which are toned down, greyed, or just plain muddy. Earth tones like ochre, rust, and khaki are obviously toned down. Gray blues, dusty pinks, and sage greens also are toned down. Once you're familiar with the idea of clarity, you probably can sort your fabrics on this dimension too, although fine degrees of clarity might be difficult to distinguish, and not worth worrying about.

Color Schemes

Generally, color schemes that include colors close to each other in hue, value, and clarity are "safer," or more likely to be pleasant, but also more likely to be unexciting. To get excitement into a color scheme, you need to have some contrast in hue, value, or clarity, but not necessarily in all three.

One standby color scheme, the basis of many old quilts, is the *monochrome*. Such a color scheme includes fabrics of different values but all one hue. Watch out for clarity in such a color scheme. If one fabric is not fitting in, it might not match the others in clarity. For instance, one clear blue in the midst of grayed blues and navies might look wrong even though its value is right. Blue Wave and Red Wave, shown in Figs. C–8 and C–6 respectively, are monochromatic quilts.

An *analogous* color scheme is one that uses hues near each other. For instance, red, orange, and yellow are near each other in the color wheel and can make a harmonious color scheme. Such a color scheme might offer built-in variations in value. In the red-orange-yellow example, yellow is naturally the lightest in value, and red the darkest. You might be able to find light reds (pinks) and light oranges (peaches) that would be as light as yellow, but it wouldn't necessarily be a good idea. The natural contrast in values probably will be an advantage to your design.

Complementary color schemes use colors from the opposite sides of the color wheel, like green and red or blue and orange. The high contrast in hue provides the oomph in the color scheme. A color scheme of equal amounts of clear, equal-value complementary hues will knock your eyes out, like op art. More often, complementary color schemes are kept under control by using more of one color than the other, by using different values of the two colors, by using toned-down versions of the two colors, or some combination of all three of these. For instance, a quilt might be mostly green with accents in red, or it might use lavender (light purple) and yellow, or it might use rust (toned-down orange) with gray blues.

Another way to dilute the effect of complementary colors is to use a lot of a neutral color along with the complementary colors. Red-and-green appliqué quilts were very common in the nineteenth century, but there was always plenty of white in these quilts to keep things under control. Value and clarity are often used to keep complementary colors under control, and might not need to be considered separately. As always, however, if something doesn't seem quite right, check for fabrics whose value or clarity might be causing the problem.

Some color schemes are based on value or clarity more than on hue. Such quilts might use all the hues, but are bound together by a common value, clarity, or both. For instance, typical depression-era quilts use many hues, but all the fabrics are light in value, and slightly toned down. The pastels typically used for baby quilts are light in value but very clear. Many old scrap quilts include fabrics in a variety of hues, generally medium to light in value, but all very toned down, whether by intention or by fading. Victorian silk quilts, including crazy quilts and log-cabin quilts, generally use rather dark, toned-down fabrics. Some contemporary quilters achieve punch with clear, mid-value rainbow colors, often supported by black. A black background intensifies the hue of mid-value colors, and intensifies the clarity of clear colors.

You might find it useful to analyze the color schemes of quilts, fabrics, paintings, or any other colored thing you like. Understanding how someone else achieved a pleasing color scheme might help you to put together your own. For example, classic Amish quilts use quite dark values, with a full range of clarity, and only part of the color wheel (green, blue, purple, red).

Color Arrangements

After you have chosen a color scheme, you still must decide how to place the colors in relation to one another. You might want to use colors to separate areas of the pattern and make each seem distinct, or you might try to achieve a blending of colors. Or, of course, you might try do both in different parts of the quilt.

In many of my quilts, particularly the one-band quilts discussed in Chapter 7, my object was to find a run of fabrics that blended together. Such runs are called *color gradations.* They can be monochrome; they can be analogous color schemes; or they can cover the whole spectrum of colors.

Blue Wave and Red Wave both have monochrome color gradations. The colors move from dark to light within one hue. There is one difference between the two quilts. In Blue Wave, the colors shade from light through medium to dark, then back through medium to light again (Fig. C–8). In Red Wave, the colors go from light through medium to dark, then switch abruptly back to light (Fig. C–6). The junction of the light and dark is the area of highest contrast and the dominant one in the quilt.

Flame Dart, shown in Fig. C–14, displays a color gradation in analogous colors. Some colors are clearer than others, but in a controlled manner. The shading from yellow to red is in rather clear colors, but the shading from red to black takes us through some toned-down reds. Thus, over all, the fabrics go from clear, light yellow to clear, mid-value red, to toned-down, very dark near-black. A toned-down orange, like a rust color, would not have fit into the sequence.

A color gradation that covers the whole spectrum, a rainbow, is very appealing. Rainbows can be constructed using colors of various values and clarities: pastel rainbows, crayon-color rainbows, deep jewel-tone rainbows. Gentle Rainbow, shown in Fig. C–7, is composed of light-value, slightly greyed colors. When you do put together a rainbow color gradation, you must be particularly careful that all the fabrics are of similar clarity, and that the values of the fabrics follow the natural sequence of values in the rainbow. That is, yellow is the lightest, purple is the darkest, and the values of the other colors shade around both sides of the color wheel. A light blue would not fit between a mid-value green and a naturally dark purple, but a royal blue would.

If you want to keep pattern areas distinct, you will need to take advantage of contrast. Contrast in value is the strongest type of contrast for this purpose. Patterns that are composed of only two fabrics, like the Ragtime quilt shown in Fig. C–10, usually use a light and a dark fabric. Fabrics of the same value, even if their hues are opposites on the color wheel, will tend to run together.

Paradoxical as it might seem, many scrap quilts are variations on the two-color quilt. For example, you can use a variety of dark fabrics in place of one dark fabric, and a variety of light fabrics in place of one light fabric. Summer/Winter Weave, shown in Fig. C–3, is an example of this approach. With this approach, you might not be able to use mid-value fabrics; in any one part of the quilt, at least, the lightest dark must be definitely darker than the darkest light.

Another scrap-quilt variation on the dark-and-light arrangement is to use one light fabric, often white or off-white, and many "dark" fabrics. Almost any fabric will seem dark when compared to white, so quilts made using this scheme can include mid-value, as well as dark, fabrics.

Scrap quilts do not need to follow a light-and-dark scheme, however. A less distinct separation of the elements of a quilt can be desirable. The Come-On quilt in Fig. C–1 and the Fused Diamonds quilt both use a variety of fabrics, but there is no organized alternation between light and dark fabrics. Some junctions between fabrics are blurry and some are sharp. This approach adds to the interest of the quilt.

Printed fabrics have pattern as well as color, and the characteristics of the pattern are often as important as the color. For instance, quilts made of fabrics that all have the same kind of pattern, even if they vary in color, tend to be boring or to have a restless, busy feeling.

The *scale* of a pattern is pretty easy to assess. How big are the flowers or other elements of the print? Scale ranges from tiny patterns, which give the impression of textures more than patterns, to the huge patterns with foot-high birds and flowers, which are used in drapery and upholstery fabrics. Try to use a range of scales in any quilt. The smaller scale patterns are many quilters' first choices. It is sometimes hard to break away from these small-scale prints, but doing so will prevent the tight, busy sameness that can afflict quilts that contain only small-scale prints.

Although very large scale fabrics can be exciting, they also can overwhelm a quilt. To decide whether a large-scale print will work in your quilt, try examining it through a *window,* a plain piece of paper with a rectangular hole in the middle. The hole should be the size of a typical piece in your quilt. Put the window on top of your large-scale print and move it around. The window might isolate interesting, usable textures, or you might find that pieces cut from different parts of the pattern would look unrelated, in which case the fabric might be less useful. Remember that you'll be using the fabric "as it comes" in the strip, and that you won't be able to pick and choose parts of the print as you might in a traditional pieced quilt.

Patterns can range in *density* from tightly packed to airy. A variety of densities, like varieties in other aspects, also can be an asset in a quilt. Extremely loose patterns might have elements that do not appear in every piece. I resisted these patterns at first, but have found that the haphazard feeling that results when a motif appears in only a few pieces can provide accents and a feeling of surprise and excitement.

Fabric patterns can have any of a number of *structures*. The most obviously different fabrics in this regard are plaids and stripes, which are favorites of mine. Plaids, in particular, often provide me with blendings of colors I find very useful. Most people think of all other patterns as *prints,* but there is a class of *stripey prints* that are somewhere between plain stripes and all-over prints.

Also related to stripes and plaids are *geometrics*. These generally have pattern elements that are not flowers or any other pictorial object, but squares, dots, triangles, lines, or other geometric shapes. More often than not, these elements are arranged in rows or on a grid, in a pattern that also seems geometric.

Most other prints are thought of as *florals,* although they might not actually contain any flowers. The elements in floral prints can be organized in clear rows or on a grid, or their repeating structure can be less obvious. If you're using a wide expanse of a floral pattern, as in a border, you might want to view it from a distance. A repeating pattern that doesn't show up at all at first glance might be glaringly obvious in a large piece and from a distance. However, such patterns probably won't matter in a pieced and pieced design, where they will be broken up.

I use fabrics with all kinds of structures and find that a variety of structures generally works in a quilt. However, pattern structure might be another thing to check when you're troubleshooting. You might have one pattern whose structure is so different from all the others that it doesn't fit. For instance, a single stripe in a group of free-form florals might not fit in. Changing a couple of the florals to intermediate types, such as stripey prints or obviously repeating florals, might bring the stripe into the blend.

COMBINING FABRICS: YOUR PERSONAL STYLE

The observations in this section are very personal. They reflect the way that I combine fabrics, and each quilter's way of combining fabrics is unique. I find it useful to learn about how other quilters work with fabrics, though, since I learn new tricks and broaden my own options.

Some quilters feel that simple one-color prints (one color and white) are easiest to deal with. I'm happier working with prints which contain at least three colors. Beginners who don't have much confidence tend to try to match fabrics too carefully, worrying about whether the green leaves in two prints are the same green. I find it easier to avoid this pitfall if I use fabrics with lots of colors in them, since I couldn't possibly match all the colors in all the prints.

For me, one sure-fire way to get a quilt going is to pick a multicolored fabric I like, and then to look for fabrics that go with it. By starting with a multicolored fabric, I open the door to many other fabrics. A new fabric need not contain all the colors in the original fabric; the two fabrics might share only one color and still seem to go together. I keep throwing candidates onto the pile until I have at least as many fabrics as I'll need. During this part of the process, I try to be wide open in my choices, and to include anything that might work.

When I've got a good heap of fabrics, I back off and see which ones stick out like sore thumbs. Some fabrics might stick out in a good way, and I don't want to discard them, just the sore thumbs. My discards are most often thrown out because of an extreme value contrast or clarity contrast.

I might need to do some more fine-tuning. If I'm trying to do a graded mono-chrome scheme, I might have gaps in value that I'll try to fill. Or I may look for bridge fabrics to pull in fabrics that I want to use, but that are too different from the rest in some way—perhaps in hue, structure, or scale. In this process, it sometimes happens that I discard the fabric I started with. That's okay. It got me started, and will eventually appear in another quilt.

I find fabrics with high value contrasts hard to work with, especially if light and dark are used in similar amounts in a busy pattern. For a while I almost swore off fabrics with white in the print because I found the bits of white distracting. I've since realized that at that time I was making quilts where all the other colors were medium to dark in value, which is why the white seemed so strong. Now I will use prints with white in a darker quilt, but I'm careful. The white is less intrusive if many of the fabrics have some white, and if the pattern uses a sparkling scattering of white, rather than big chunks of white.

Combining solids and prints seems to be a stumbling block for many quilters, including myself. When I made my first traditional quilts, I tended to use solids and prints as though I were coloring a map. I followed an unconscious rule that print couldn't touch print and solid couldn't touch solid. Such rules can help the visual separation of pieces, but are terribly limiting. There are other contrasts you can use to keep pieces distinct, if that's desired.

In fact, I've found myself going overboard in the opposite direction. I've made all-solid quilts and all-print quilts, but seldom combined the two. In traditional quilts where the pattern is composed of a figure on a background, the background often will be a solid, while the figure is a print. This is a straightforward way to combine the two kinds of fabrics. In most pieced and repieced quilts, there is no obvious background, and I find solids difficult to incorporate. I do use *near-solids,* however. These are fabrics with a very slight pattern, and little contrast in value between the colors in the fabric.

Color and fabric selection can be the most difficult part of quilting. Learning about color characteristics, color schemes, and pattern characteristics can help, though often in a backwards, analytical way. If a quilt goes wrong, you can use these ideas to figure out how it went wrong. Luckily, a quilt doesn't have to be complete before you can analyze it. When a quilt is still a heap of fabric, or still a pile of strips, but doesn't look right, you can run through a mental checklist of these elements to try to identify what's wrong.

So if these principles are mainly useful for picking fabric combinations apart, how do you go forward to put combinations together? The answer is to put things together by "feel" or by "intuition." This doesn't seem like much of an answer at first, but I think that it's the only real answer. You already have a feeling for color and pattern, however limited. You choose clothing for yourself and make decorating choices about the place you live, whether it's choosing a poster or two for a dorm room or creating a coordinated decor for a whole house.

Start with that feeling, and build. It will be a building process: you'll have to start simple and work up to sophisticated color schemes. For your first quilt, use something straightforward you know you like. Choose a rainbow of pastels, or use all blue-and-white prints, or all earth tones. Your first quilt will not be a miracle of sophisticated color and fabric merging, unless you've developed these skills in some other area, but it should be something you like.

For later quilts, the size of the steps you take will depend on your personality. If you like to feel safe and secure, take a look at your last quilt, and think of a little variation you could make that would spice it up a bit. The variation might or might not work out the way you expected, but if it's a small part of the overall scheme of the quilt, you'll still have a good-looking quilt even if your experiment didn't succeed. You can build on the success of your previous quilts, taking small steps to develop your style. Your quilts will not cover a broad area, but should be satisfying.

If you want to take larger strides, you'll need to take greater risks. Some of your quilts might not work out, and you might develop a pile of unfinished rejects. However, you're more likely to get to exciting results faster.

Do try to build, though, rather than dashing around aimlessly. Return to quilts that worked and try to make similar quilts that also work well. I used to feel than all my quilts had to be completely different from each other. It was a relief and a pleasure to find that, in the art quilting world, it is not only acceptable but fashionable to work *in a series.* In other words, many quilting ideas can't be worked out completely the first time. A series of several quilts, all on the same lines, might be more satisfactory for you to make, and also might be more interesting, as a group, to others.

Chapter 7
One-Band
Shift Patterns

The patterns in this chapter are related to bargello needlepoint patterns, a kind of needlepoint that enjoyed a surge of popularity a few years ago, partly because of its ease in working. In bargello, all stitches are simple upright stitches, usually all of the same length. Starting in the first color, and following the directions carefully, you lay out a foundation row. After the foundation row is in place, other rows in other colors simply follow the first. The dark row at the bottom of Fig. 7–1 is the foundation row.

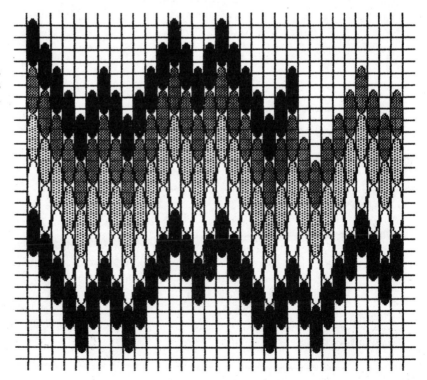

Fig. 7–1. This detail shows how bargello needlepoint is constructed.

We'll borrow the term *row* from bargello. In our pieced patterns, a row is an area made up of rectangles cut from any one fabric, and usually runs horizontally across the quilt.

You can achieve bargellolike effects easily in piecing and repiecing, as was explained briefly in Chapter 1. Because all rows are the same, only one band is needed.

THE LOOP-AND-SHIFT TECHNIQUE

One additional technique, called *looping and shifting,* is needed for making these patterns. The shifting is the part that produces the pattern, while the looping is the part that allows you to shift without wasting any fabric. The simple Zigzag pattern (Fig. 7 – 2) illustrates the basic technique. Further refinements and points that arise in more complex patterns are covered in the general discussion following the example.

Zigzag

Choose the fabrics you want to use (Table 7 – 1) and make a working drawing of the pattern, colored so that you can tell which fabric goes where. Draw in the grid on your drawing, at least across the top part. It will be important for you to be able to see the sizes of the rectangles at the top edge of the pattern. Figure 7 – 3 shows the pattern area for a Zigzag quilt with the colors that will be referred to in the following discussion.

Cut the strips and mark the cross-cut lines using a template marked every 1½ inches. Assemble the strips into the one band needed and cut your first segment from the band.

Table 7 – 1. Strips for Zigzag Quilt.

GRID SIZE: **1**″ Finished Size of Pattern Area: **33**″ × **47 1/2**″

Each of 12 fabrics   1 @ 49 1/2″ × 4 1/2″

SHOPPING LIST
    Fabric
      1-12: 1/4 yard 45″ wide fabric.
    Border: For unpieced border, 1 5/8 yards fabric.
           For pieced 4″ border, 3/4 yard 45″ wide fabric.
    Backing: If backing fabric is wider than quilt top, 1 5/8 yards.
           If backing fabric is narrower than quilt top, 2 3/4 yards.
    Batting: About 50″ × 60″.
    Binding: About 5 5/8 yards of 1 1/2″ binding. Can be purchased or cut from 1/4 yard fabric. If backing is made from fabric narrower than the quilt top, there will be enough extra fabric for binding.

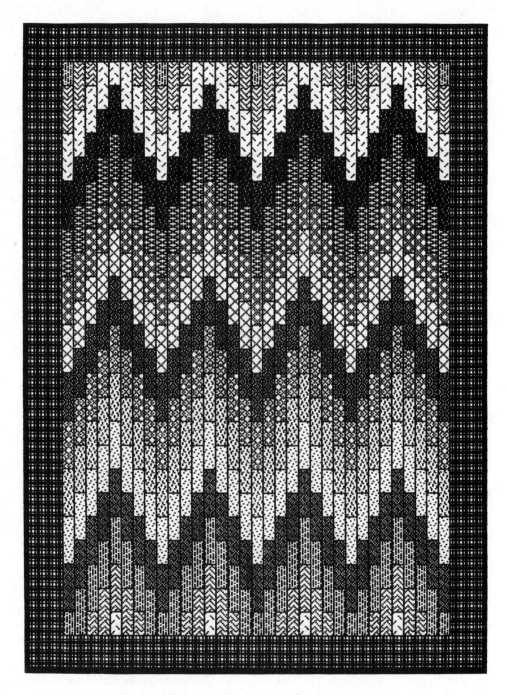

Fig. 7–2. The Zigzag quilt has a simple one-band pattern.

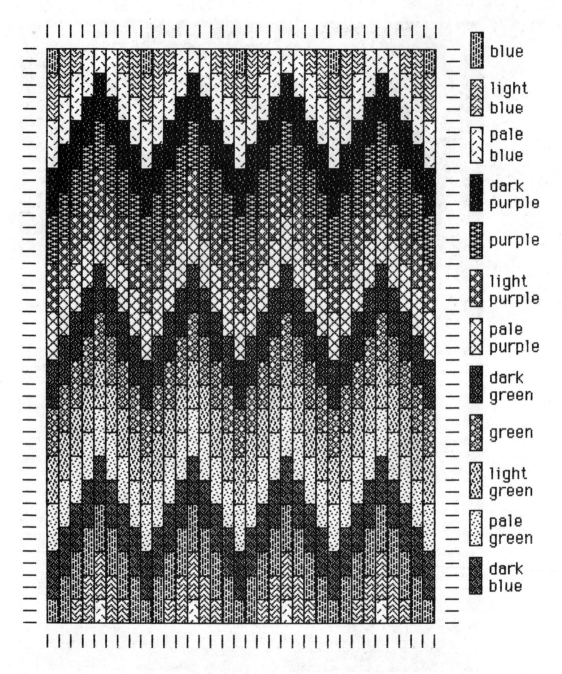

Fig. 7–3. The construction drawing includes labels for the colors used in the instructions for the Zigzag quilt. The tick marks can be used to draw a 1-inch grid.

Sew the two ends of the first segment together, forming a loop. Now look at your drawing, at the top of the leftmost segment of the pattern. The rectangle in the top left corner of the pattern is blue, and is 1 inch wide and 2 inches tall. Find the blue rectangle in the segment. It's 4 inches tall, from seam to seam. To get the 2-inch-tall rectangle you want, measure 2 inches from one of the seams and cut across the blue rectangle. Lay the first segment out flat. It should look like the first segment in the diagram. Note that the other half of the blue rectangle ends up at the bottom of the quilt.

If you're keeping track of seam allowances, you might wonder whether the blue rectangle should have been cut 2¼ inches from the seam. The answer is no, since if the rectangle at the top of the quilt had an additional ¼ inch to allow for a seam allowance, the rectangle at the bottom of the quilt would have been shortened by this ¼ inch. When you sew a border to the pattern area, you will, in fact, cut ¼ inch of the pattern from each end. Trying to allow for seam allowances would destroy the economy of the shift and loop method, so I just live with this curtailment, which is slight enough so that it is seldom noticed.

Cut the next segment and loop it. You'll see that the second segment in the drawing has a 1-X-4-inch light blue rectangle at the top of the quilt. Because the light blue part of the segment is 4 inches between seams, you'll cut the loop right at one of the seams. Be sure that it's the right seam. The pale blue rectangle is right below the light blue one in the drawing, so that's not the seam to cut; cut at the seam between the light blue and the blue. Make this cut by turning over to the back of the segment and cutting right along the stitching of the seam.

Another word about seam allowances. I've just directed you to cut off the seam allowances of the seam that held the light and medium blue rectangles together. Couldn't you just remove the stitching, and save the seam allowances? If you did, this segment would end up 36½ inches long, while the first was only 36 inches long. You really do need to cut off those little bits of seam allowance.

Sew the second segment to the first. Cut and loop the third segment. This loop will be cut in the middle of the light blue rectangle. Sew the third segment to the

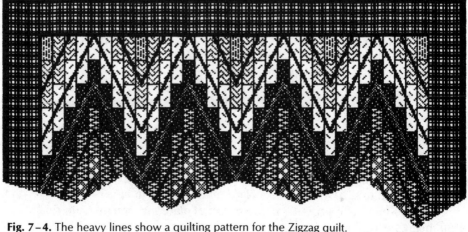

Fig. 7–4. The heavy lines show a quilting pattern for the Zigzag quilt.

second. Cut and loop the fourth segment, then cut it at the seam between the light blue and the pale blue. Sew the fourth segment to the third. Continue in this way until the pattern area is complete.

Quilt Zigzag by following the zigs and zags, as shown in Fig. 7 – 4. This method of quilting emphasizes the design and is easy to mark. In each seam between two segments, two rectangles of the same fabric overlap by 2 inches. The quilting crosses the seam in the center of this overlap. To mark the design, measure the overlap, which ought to be 2 inches, but might be slightly different, and place a small horizontal tick mark in the center of the overlap. When you've made several tick marks, use a ruler to connect the marks and draw the quilting line.

General Directions for Looping and Shifting

In Zigzag, all the places in which loops are cut are either on a seam or halfway between seams. With some other patterns, a cut might be closer to one seam than the other. Measure the correct distance, check to be sure you measured from the proper end of the rectangle, then cut. If you should make the cut and then discover you've measured from the wrong end of the rectangle, all is not lost. Pick out the stitching holding the two pieces of the rectangle to the rest of the segment, then switch the two pieces and sew them back in place. If you cut in a completely wrong place, you need only to replace the one miscut rectangle.

Machine piecers get involved in *chaining,* which is a way of working that lets you sew seam after seam without breaking off the thread. This saves a little thread, and also can be helpful in developing a smooth-running routine that will minimize errors. With shift patterns, I chain as follows. Cut the first segment, loop it, and leave it on the sewing machine, under the presser foot. Cut the second segment and loop it, again leaving it on the machine. The first two loops are now connected by a pair of threads and form the first two pieces of the chain. Cut the third segment, loop it, and leave it in the chain. Snip the stitching that connects the first loop to the chain and make the cut in the first loop. Snip the second loop from the chain and make the cut in the second loop. Sew the second segment to the first segment.

At this point, the pattern area is started, though it's only two segments wide. The next loop needed is in the chain, connected to the top of the pattern area. Now the chain has been set up, and we'll come back to this point after each step in the routine.

Cut the fourth segment from the band, and loop it. Snip the third loop from the top of the chain and make the cut in it. Snip the pattern area from the chain and sew the third segment to the pattern area. Continue in this way for the remaining segments: cut a segment and loop it; snip off the previous loop and make the cut in it; snip the pattern area from the chain; sew the segment to the pattern area.

Double Peaks

There are many variations on a simple zigzag, some of which are illustrated in Fig. 7 – 5. One of these zigzags is the same as the bargello design illustrated in Fig. 7 – 1 and is also used in the Double Peaks place mats (Figs. 7 – 6 and 7 – 7).

The 264-inch-long strips required for a set of place mats might seem ridiculous. You might, instead, cut a set of strips for each place mat, as indicated in the second

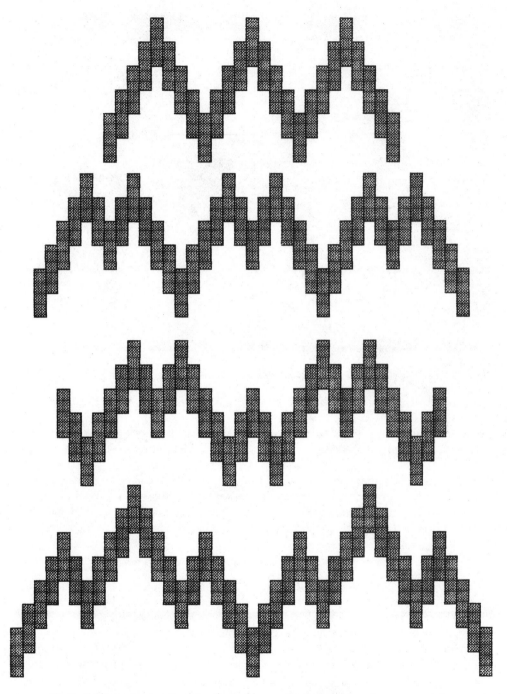

Fig. 7–5. These zigzag patterns are formed by varying the numbers of steps up and down.

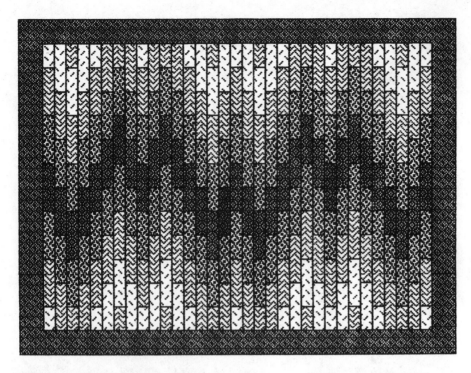

Fig. 7 – 6. These place mats in the Double Peaks pattern use a one-band pattern that is slightly more complicated than the simple Zigzag.

column of Table 7 – 2. If you do, you might want to cut your fabric to a little over 33 inches wide before you cut strips, rather than cutting stripping the full width of the fabric.

You'll need a paper template marked every 1 inch. You can choose to quilt the place mats or not, and you can use the quilt method or the pillow method to construct them. Instructions for both methods of constructing place mats are given in Chapter 3. If you decide to quilt the place mats, use a quilting pattern like that for Zigzag.

CREATING CURVES BY VARYING SEGMENT WIDTHS

The zigzag patterns we've been looking at can be varied by using segments of different widths. Varying segment widths can create the illusion of curves. The variations in Fig. 7 – 8 are variations on a simple zigzag. The more complicated zigzags in Fig. 7 – 5 also can be varied by using segments of different widths.

If you look in bargello books for inspiration, you'll find that many of the patterns use blocks of stitches that correspond to segments of varying widths. Some of the more interesting ones have repeats of 40 to 80 stitches. I usually base my quilts on a 1-inch grid, so if I used the needlepoint design directly, I would have a piecing pattern that repeated every 40 to 80 inches. This is too big a pattern for most of my work, so I usually simplify the pattern, trying to capture its effect in a smaller number of segments.

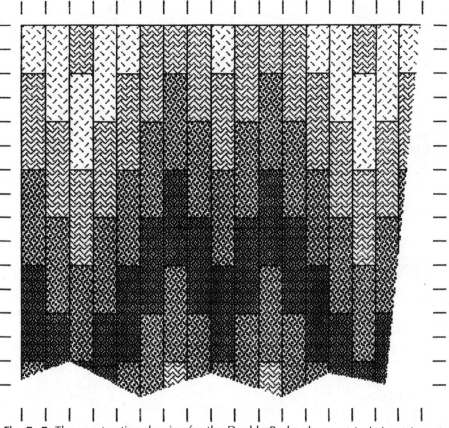

Fig. 7–7. The construction drawing for the Double Peaks place mat includes tick marks for drawing a ½-inch grid.

Table 7–2. Strips for Double Peaks Place Mats, Set of Eight.

GRID SIZE: **1/2″** Finished Size of Pattern Area: **11 1/2″ × 16 1/2″**

Darkest and Lightest Fabrics	1 @ 264″ × 2 1/2″	or 8 @ 33 × 2 1/2″
Each of 2 Intermediate Fabrics	2 @ 264″ × 2 1/2″	or 16 @ 33 × 2 1/2″

SHOPPING LIST

Darkest and Lightest Fabrics: 5/8 yard 36″ or 45″ wide fabric.

Each of 2 Intermediate Fabrics: 1 1/8 yards 36″ or 45″ wide fabric.

Border: 5/8 yard 45″ wide fabric.

Backing: 2 yards 45″ wide fabric.

Batting: Optional. If used for ''quilt'' method, eight pieces 16″ × 21″. If used for ''pillow'' method, eight pieces 14″ × 19″.

Binding: Optional. If used, about 14 1/2 yards of 1 1/2″ binding. Can be purchased or cut from 5/8 yard of 45″ wide fabric.

Fig. 7–8. All these patterns are based on the Zigzag shown at the top. The arabesque, sinuous line, arch, and swag variations are created by using segments of different widths.

Gentle Rainbow

The Gentle Rainbow quilt, shown in Fig. C–7, uses a simplified version of one element from a complicated bargello design that repeated every 73 stitches. The segments in Gentle Rainbow are 1, 2, 3, or 5 inches wide (Fig. 7–9). Note that the 4-inch segment you'd expect has been left out. (See Table 7–3.)

The strips are a little too long to fit across 45-inch fabric, so you'll need to cut the tag ends separately. The directions call for ⅜ yard of material in each color. Since ⅛ yard is 4½ inches, this would be exactly the right amount of material to cut three pieces of stripping across the width of the fabric if the yardage were cut exactly straight, which it might not be. Even if the fabric is cut crooked, however, so that you cannot cut three pieces of stripping, you can cut two pieces and a couple of short bits.

Because the segments in Gentle Rainbow are not all of the same width, you'll need to make a paper template especially for this quilt. The template should be marked as follows:

1½, 3, 4½, 6, 7½, 9, 10½, 12, 14½, 16, 19½, 25 (center segment), 28½, 31, 33½, 35, 36½, 38, 39½, 41, 42½, 44, 45½

Quilt Gentle Rainbow with lines that follow each fabric, as in Zigzag or Double Peaks, and with parallel lines that follow the joins between rows. The quilting along the joins is needed because the pattern row contains gentle curves, as well as steep zigzags. The lines of quilting are farther apart where the pattern row curves, so the extra quilting is necessary to keep the quilting lines from being too far apart.

The quilting design is marked in the same way that Zigzag was marked, by making tick marks halfway up overlaps. Joining the tick marks produces a quilting pattern composed of a number of straight lines. As you do the quilting, you can smooth out the angles where the lines meet, so that the finished quilted line is, in fact, curved.

The one part of the quilting line that's actually marked as a curve is the bit at the top of the arch. Figure 7–10 shows how to join the tick marks at the sides of the segment with a curve that graves a horizontal guideline. It doesn't matter if the curve is a little wobbly; it will naturally tend to straighten out as you do the quilting.

CREATING CURVES BY VARYING OFFSETS

Another way to create curved effects is to vary the offsets between segments. So far, the offset between segments has always been half the height of a rectangle. Figure 7–11 shows variations on a simple zigzag achieved by varying offsets.

The Vaults

The Vaults (Table 7–4 and Figs. C–11 and C–20), is a variation on the arabesque shown in Fig. 7–12. The three "vaults" in the pattern are not quite the same; the center point is higher than the others.

I made this quilt in a variety of nontraditional fabrics, including velvet, wool, and a shiny synthetic. These fabrics did not lend themselves to the usual shaded color scheme. Instead, I tried various arrangements, then decided on a sequence I liked.

Table 7–3. Strips for Gentle Rainbow Quilt.

GRID SIZE: **1″** Finished Size of Pattern Area: **35″ × 55 1/2″**

Each of 7 fabrics   2 @ 46 1/2″ × 4 1/2″

SHOPPING LIST
Each fabric   1/4 yard 45″ wide fabric.
Inner Border: 1/4 yard 45″ wide fabric.
Border: For unpieced borders, 1 7/8 yards fabric.
For pieced 5″ border, 3/4 yards 45″ wide fabric.
Backing: For fabric wider than quilt top, 1 7/8 yards.
For fabric narrower than quilt top, 2 5/8 yards.
Batting: About 50″ × 70″.
Binding: About 4 1/4 yards of 1 1/2″ binding. Can be purchased or cut from 3/8
yards fabric. If inner border and binding are cut from same fabric, 1/2
yard 45″ fabric will be sufficient for both.

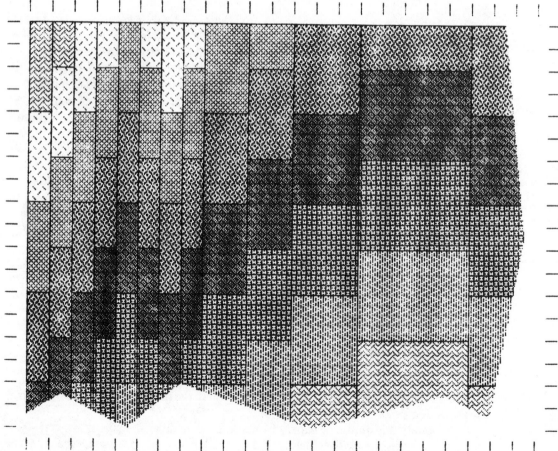

Fig. 7–9. The construction diagram for the Gentle Rainbow quilt includes tick marks for drawing a 1-inch grid.

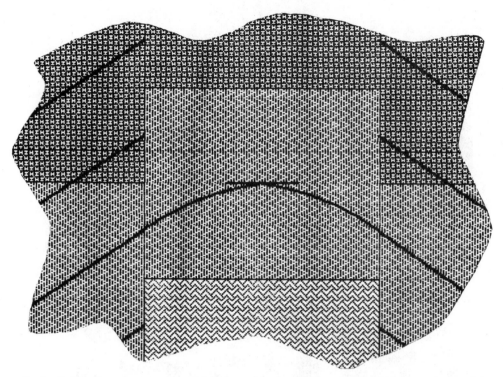

Fig. 7–10. This close-up shows the guidelines used for drawing the curved quilting line at the top of the arch. The quilting line just touches a line halfway up the top rectangle.

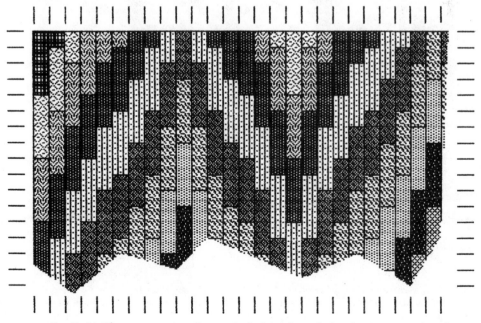

Fig. 7–11. The construction diagram includes tick marks for drawing a 1-inch grid.

109

Fig. 7–12. These patterns are all based on the simple zigzag at the top. The arabesque, sinuous line, swag, and arch variations shown here are achieved by varying the overlap between rectangles of the same color.

Table 7–4. Strips for The Vaults Quilt.

GRID SIZE: **1**″ Finished Size of Pattern Area: **51**″ × **39 1/2**″

Each of 10 fabrics   1 @ 76 1/2″ × 4 1/2″

SHOPPING LIST
Each fabric: 3/8 yard 45″ wide fabric.
   Border: For unpieced border, 1 3/4 yards fabric.
           For pieced, abutted 5″ border, 7/8 yard 45″ wide fabric.
  Backing: For fabric wider than quilt top, 1 3/4 yards fabric.
           For fabric narrower than quilt top, 2 7/8 yards fabric.
  Batting: About 54″ × 65″.
  Binding: About 6 1/4 yards of 2″ binding. Can be purchased or cut from 3/8 yard of fabric.

The next step was to choose which fabrics to place in the center of the quilt, where they would flow, unbroken. Fabrics placed on the edges of the quilt form rows that run off the top of the quilt, then back on the bottom of the quilt, or vice versa. It's a good idea to have one of your strongest fabrics, which might be the darkest, the lightest, or the brightest, as a prominent unbroken row.

    I used a 2-inch binding in my quilt because I was working with heavier fabrics. If you use regular quilt-weight fabrics, a 1½-inch binding should be wide enough.

OTHER VARIATIONS

The basic building blocks for shift patterns are zigzags, varying segment widths, and varying offsets. Varying offsets and varying widths can be used together, as in the Blue Wave and Shazam quilts discussed in this section.

    Other variations are possible, as well. In all the other patterns in this chapter, rows that go off the top of the quilt come back on the bottom, and vice versa. The Swags album cover displays a sneaky way around this limitation. Flame Dart breaks another unwritten rule. All other quilts in this chapter are based on strips of only one width, but Flame Dart has broad and narrow strips in each color.

Blue Wave

    Blue Wave (Table 7–5 and Figs. C–8, C–19, and 7–13) achieves its curves primarily with varying offsets. However, the bends in the rows are softened by the use of double-width segments. A segment of double width also can be thought of as two segments with a "zero" offset between them. You'll need a special paper template, marked as follows.

        1½, 3, 4½, 6, 7½, 10 (1st wide segment),
        11½, 13, 14½, 16, 17½, 19, 20½, 22, 23½, 26 (2nd wide segment),
        27½, 29, 30½, 32, 33½, 35, 36½, 38, 39½, 42 (3rd wide segment),
        43½, 45, 46½, 48, 49½, 51, 52½, 54, 55½, 58 (4th wide segment),
        59½, 61, 62½, 64, 65½

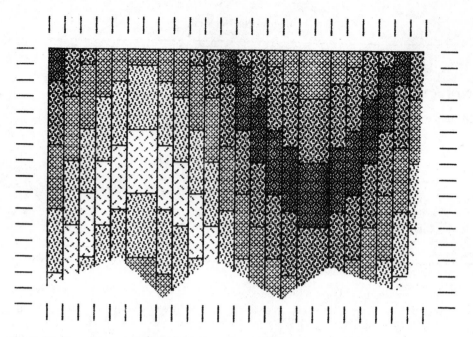

Fig. 7–13. The construction diagram for Blue Wave includes tick marks for drawing a 1-inch grid.

Table 7–5. Strips for Blue Wave Quilt.

GRID SIZE: **1"** Finished Size of Pattern Area: **45" × 63 1/2"**

Lightest and Darkest Fabrics	2 @ 65 1/2" × 4 1/2"
Each of 3 Intermediate Fabrics	4 @ 65 1/2" × 4 1/2"

SHOPPING LIST

Darkest and Lightest Fabrics: 7/8 yard 45" wide fabric.

Each of 3 Intermediate
Fabrics: 1 5/8 yards 45" wide fabric.

Border: For unpieced border, 1 7/8 yards fabric.
For pieced 1" border, 1/4 yard fabric.

Backing: For fabric wider than quilt top, 1 7/8 yards fabric
For fabric narrower than quilt top, 2 3/4 yards fabric

Batting: About 50" × 70".

Binding: About 6 3/8 yards 1 1/2" binding. Can be purchased or cut
from 3/8 yard fabric.

The quilting pattern for Blue Wave is much like that for Gentle Rainbow. Only one line of quilting is used for each row, however, since the curves in Blue Wave are tighter than those in Gentle Rainbow. This was one of my earliest bargello quilts, and has the narrow border I was using at that time. If I were making this quilt today, I might use a wider border, but the simple, narrow border also has its appeal.

Shazam

Bargello patterns need not repeat horizontally, or even be symmetrical from side to side. Shazam (Table 7–6 and Figs. C–18 and 7–14) demonstrates that repeats and symmetry are not necessary. It does use both varying offsets and varying widths extensively. It was designed by my husband as a gift for his brother. Allen felt free to "break the rules" I used—rules about using either width variations or offset variations alone—since he didn't know what the rules were. The result is a freer, more dynamic design than I would have come up with on my own.

The original quilt used seven fabrics, one for each of the rainbow colors: red, orange, yellow, green, blue, indigo, and violet. Another rule has been broken in the arrangement of the colors, however. The fabrics are arranged red, orange, yellow, violet, indigo, blue, green, rather than in their rainbow order. Note how the strong yellow row runs unbroken across the quilt. The quilting for Shazam is "the usual," except for one tricky spot, noted in Fig. 17–15.

The special paper template required for this quilt should be marked as follows.

1½, 3, 4½, 6, 7½, 9, 10½, 13, 16½, 21 (widest segment),
22½, 24, 25½, 27, 28½, 30, 31½, 33, 34½, 36, 38½ (top of arch),
40, 41½, 43, 44½, 46, 47½, 49, 50½, 52, 54½ (bottom of swag),
57, 58½, 60, 61½, 63, 64½, 66, 67½, 69, 70½

Table 7–6. Strips for Shazam Quilt.

GRID SIZE: **1**″ Finished Size of Pattern Area: **50″ × 27 1/2″**

Each of 7 fabrics   1 @ 70 1/2″ × 4 1/2″

SHOPPING LIST
Each fabric: 3/8 yard 36″ or 45″ wide fabric.
   Border: For unpieced borders, 1 5/8 yards fabric.
           For pieced, 5″ border, 7/8 yard 45″ wide fabric.
  Backing: 1 5/8 yards 45″ wide fabric.
  Batting: About 42″ × 60″.
  Binding: About 5 3/8 yards of 1 1/2″ binding. Can be purchased or cut from 1/4 yard of 45″ fabric.

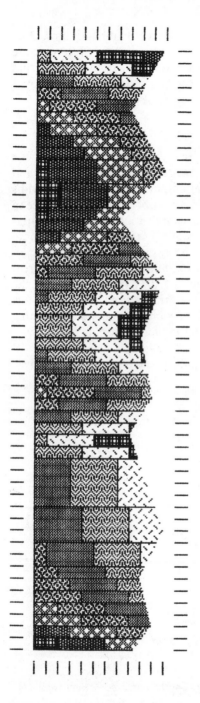

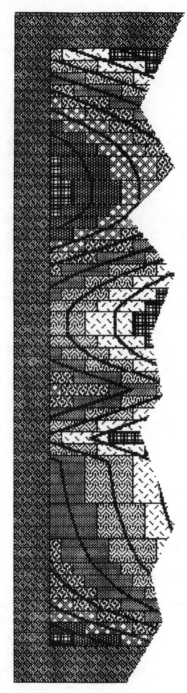

Fig. 7–15. The quilting pattern for Shazam shows the area where the zigzag meets the top of the curve. The zigzag continues down to a point halfway between the top and bottom of the square. Mark the quilting line from this point to the center of the offset on the left edge of the square.

Fig. 7–14. The construction diagram for the Shazam quilt includes tick marks for drawing a 1-inch grid. The drawing has been turned 90 degrees.

114

Swags

The Swags pattern is shown as a cover for an album or notebook in Fig. 7–16. Swags uses varying offsets and a triple-wide segment for the turn-around in the curve. Its principal feature is that it uses a background fabric (Table 7–7). All the pattern strips are the same width, but the background strip is much wider. Because the background strip is so wide, all the loops can be cut within the background fabric, allowing all the pattern rows to be unbroken.

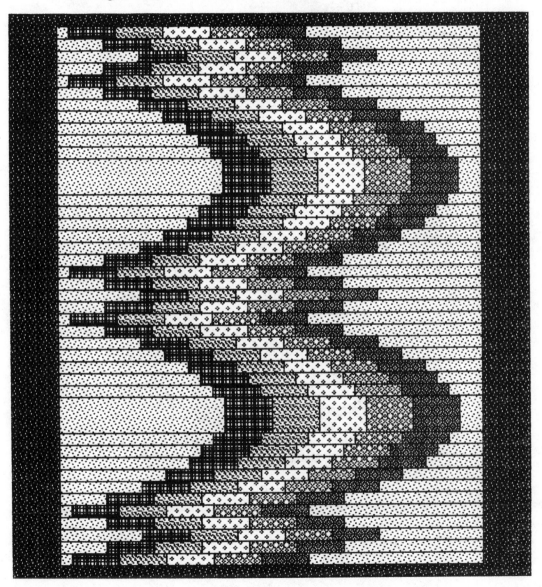

Fig. 7–16. This notebook cover uses the Swags pattern, which uses varying offsets, a triple-wide segment, and an extra-wide ''background'' strip.

115

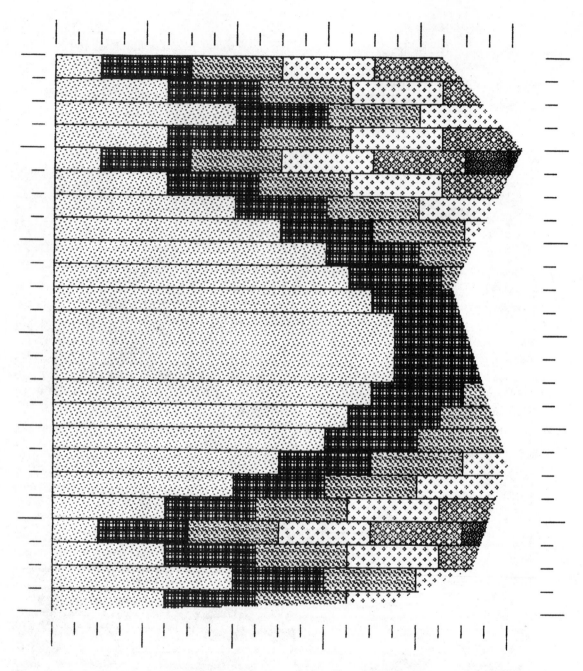

Fig. 7–17. The construction diagram for the Swags pattern includes tick marks for drawing a ¼-inch grid.

Table 7-7. Strips for Swags Album Cover.

GRID SIZE: **1/4″** Finished Size of Pattern Area: **9″ × 11 1/4″**

Each of 5 Fabrics	1 @ 31 3/4″ × 1 1/2″
Background Fabric	1 @ 31 3/4″ × 4 1/2″

SHOPPING LIST
    Each of 5 Fabrics: Scraps.
    Background Fabric: 3/8 yard 36″ or 45″ wide fabric.
    Cover Fabric: 3/4 yard 36″ or 45″ wide fabric.

The size of the album cover will depend on the size of the album, but should be larger than the pattern area. If the album is less than 11¼ inches tall, try leaving off the last two segments on either end of the pattern area.

Like all patterns with segments of varying widths, it needs a special paper template. This one is marked as follows.

¾, 1½, 2¼, 3, 3¾, 4½, 5¼, 6, 6¾, 7½, 8.25, 9½ (wide segment)
10¼, 11, 11¾, 12½, 13¼, 14, 14¾, 15½, 16¼ (center segment)
17, 17¾, 18½, 19¼, 20, 20¾, 21½, 22¼, 23½ (wide segment)
24¼, 25, 25¾, 26½, 27¼, 28, 28¾, 29½ 30¼, 31, 31¾

When the pattern area is complete, add borders, like those shown in Fig. 7-18, to make the cover. The size of the borders depends on the size of the album. The first borders to add are those that extend the pattern area to the needed height, ½ inch greater than the height of the notebook. When the borders in the other direction are added, the entire album cover "top" should be ½ inch longer than the measurement from the front edge of the album around the spine to the back edge.

The next step is to make the flaps that will go over the insides of the cover. Their height will be the same as the cover top, and their width slightly less than the width of the front cover of the album. Finish one long edge of each flap with a narrow hem.

We need one more piece: the lining for the spine. Measure the spine and add about 2 inches to allow for overlap between the flaps and the spine lining. Place the lining on top of the flaps, right side down, as shown in Fig. 7-19. Sew all around the edges, using a quarter-inch seam.

Turn the cover inside out. The spine lining will be "inside" the flaps. Bend the covers of the album back and slip the flaps over the covers. The cloth cover should stretch enough to go over the thickness of the album. If the cloth cover is too loose, turn it back inside out and sew another seam inside the first one to take up the slack.

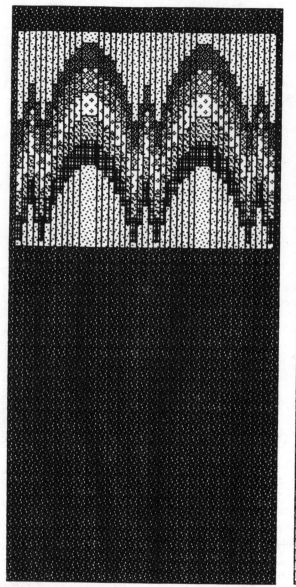

Fig. 7–18. Borders are added to the Swags pattern area to create the outside of the notebook cover.

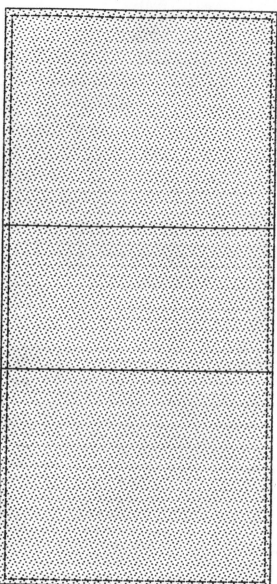

Fig. 7–19. The spine liner has been placed right side down on top of the inside flaps. Sew all around the edges, as shown by the dotted line.

118

Flame Dart

One of my rules for designing shift patterns has been that colors had to "connect" from segment to segment. Whenever I thought about using some broad and some narrow strips, I thought I would be limited to offsets no bigger than the width of the narrow strips. Flame Dart, shown in Fig. C–14, satisfies my requirement that colors connect, but still uses offsets greater than the width of the narrow strips.

To see how this works, cover up most of Fig. 7–20 and look at only one segment. For each color, the broad strip is separated from the narrow strips by only 1 inch. The three-inch offset between segments means that squares that come from the narrow strip are connected to rectangles that come from the broad strip. The only squares left unconnected are at the point of the V.

Strips will just fit on most 45-inch fabrics (Table 7–8). My Flame Dart quilt has a narrow inner border that is about 1 inch wide — not quite as narrow as most other inner borders in this book. Your choice will depend on the particular fabrics you're using. Use a quilting pattern of straight lines that run through the centers of the overlaps of rectangles with rectangles.

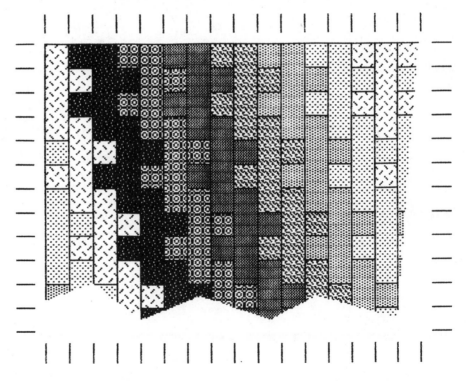

Fig. 7–20. The construction diagram for the Flame Dart quilt includes tick marks for drawing a 1-inch grid.

Table 7–8. Strips for Flame Dart Quilt.

GRID SIZE: **1**″ Finished Size of Pattern Area: **29 1/2**″ × **41 1/2**″

Each of 7 Fabrics   1 @ 43 1/2″ × 4 1/2″
                    2 @ 43 1/2″ × 1 1/2″

SHOPPING LIST
    Each Fabric: 1/4 yard 45″ wide fabric.
   Inner Border: 1/4 yard 45″ wide fabric.
        Border: For mitered border, 1 1/2 yards fabric.
                For abutted 4″ border, 5/8 yard 45″ wide fabric.
      Backing: 1 1/2 yards 45″ wide fabric.
      Batting: About 43″ × 56″.
      Binding: About 5 1/8 yards 1 1/2″ binding. Can be purchased or cut from 1/4 yard fabric.

Chapter 8
Shifted Multiple-Band Patterns

The first two patterns in this chapter are variations on multiple-band patterns. The first, Plus Signs, is made with the bands from our old friend Come-On. Ziggurats is a three-band pattern. The next and largest group of patterns are *half-drop patterns,* patterns that look like they were laid out on a diamond-shaped grid. Finally we have two patterns that are based on Hungarian Point needlepoint and look more like the shift patterns in Chapter 7. All the patterns in this chapter are quilts, and many are full-size (bed size) quilts. This reflects the fact that the patterns in this chapter are generally larger in scale than those in earlier chapters.

Plus Signs

When I teach pieced and repieced quilts in a half-day workshop, we don't have time for the students to make cloth quilts. Instead, we work with colored construction paper. We mimic the sewing process, cutting strips of paper, "sewing" them together with tape, then cutting the bands into segments, and arranging the paper segments into patterns. One day in class, I was fooling around with a bunch of paper Come-On segments like those for the sorter-armed Come-On used in the place mats. I put together a group of three segments, ABA, and noticed that I got a plus sign. When you continue the Come-On pattern in the usual way, this plus sign runs together with others and gets lost in the pattern, but I wanted to keep the figure distinct. So I put another ABA group of segments down next to the first, but shifted it, so that the plus signs would stay separate.

The row in the Plus Signs pattern shown in Figs. 8–1 and 8–2 goes down, then up, then down. This could be varied, of course, to an overall V pattern, or an M or a W, or any other sort of zigzag scheme.

Note that one difference between Plus Signs and the parent Come-On pattern is that Plus Signs uses twice as many A band segments as B band segments. Thus, the strips for the A Band are twice as long as the strips for the B Band.

You'll start the chain for the quilt by looping an A segment, then a B segment, then an A segment. Cut the first A loop and the B loop, and sew them together. At this point, your chain contains the barely begun pattern area, consisting of only two segments and the second looped A segment. You'll sew that looped A segment into the pattern area next, so you need to think to the step beyond that in deciding what segment to cut from the band next. It will be another A segment. Continue in this manner, thinking ahead one step in cutting segments to loop.

The Plus Signs quilt as shown uses 24 different fabrics — 12 light and 12 dark — and was meant to be a scrap quilt (Table 8–1). You also could use three rows of each of 4 dark and 4 light fabrics or use 12, 6, or 4 fabrics, or even in just 1 light and 1 dark fabric.

The quilting pattern for Plus Signs goes through the centers of the light squares. Locate these centers, then use a ruler to draw lines connecting them. The quilting line should stay within the light-colored fabrics, crossing the seam near the corner of the dark-colored rectangle ⅙ inch from the plus.

Table 8–1. Strips for Plus Signs Quilt.

GRID SIZE: **1 1/2"** Finished Size of Pattern Area: **54" × 71 1/2"**

	BAND A **(48" strips)**	BAND B **(24" strips)**
Each of 12 dark fabrics	1 @ 2" × 48"	1 @ 5" × 24"
Each of 12 light fabrics	1 @ 5" × 48"	1 @ 2" × 24"

SHOPPING LIST

Each Fabric: 1/4 yard 45" fabric.

Border: For borders less than about 11" wide, 2 3/4 yards 45" wide fabric.

Backing: 5 1/2 yards 45" wide fabric.

Batting: About 78" × 96".

Binding: About 9 1/4 yards of 1 1/2" binding. Can be purchased or cut from 3/8 yard of fabric.

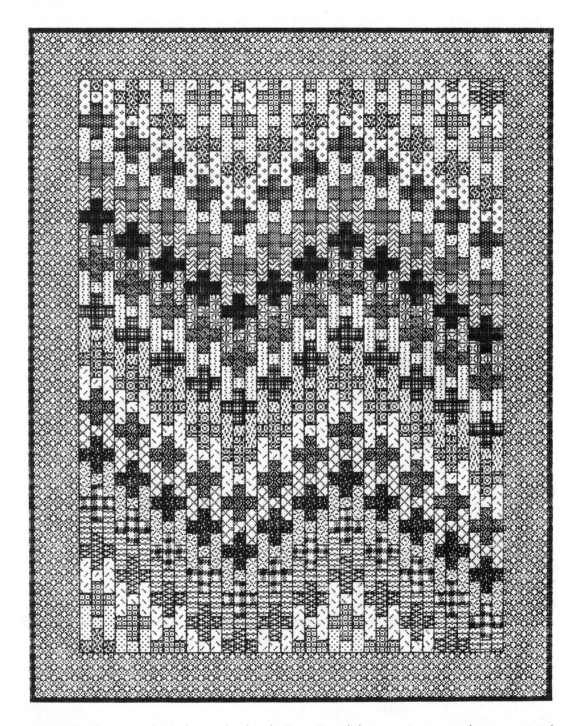

Fig. 8–1. The Plus Signs quilt uses the same bands as the Come-On quilt, but uses twice as many of one segment as of the other, and uses shifting as well.

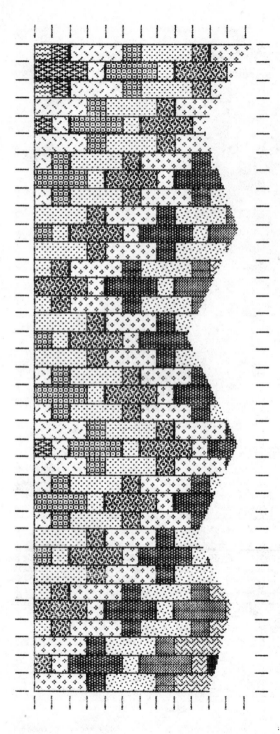

Fig. 8–2. The construction diagram for the Plus Signs quilt has been turned 90 degrees. The tick marks can be used to draw a 1½-inch grid.

Ziggurats

Ziggurats is a three-band pattern with segments placed horizontally in the quilt. (See Fig. 8–3, and Table 8–2.) Groups of three segments shift alternately to the right and left, creating a larger pattern that repeats every six segments. The stair-step effect on the edges of the pattern reminded me of the Babylonian step pyramids called *ziggurats*. This is another pattern that could be done in just two fabrics, one light and one dark.

Fig. 8–3. The construction diagram for the Ziggurats quilt includes tick marks for drawing a 1½-inch grid. Because the segments in the quilt are horizontal, construction starts at the lower left corner of the quilt, rather than the upper left corner.

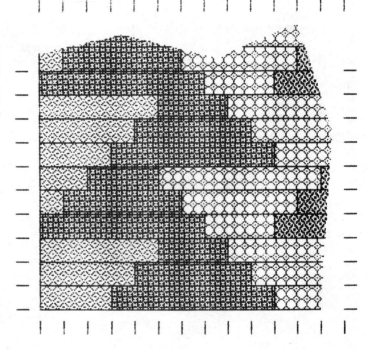

Table 8–2. Strips for Ziggurats Quilt.

GRID SIZE: **1 1/2″** Finished Size of Pattern Area: **29 1/2″ × 36″**

	BAND A (16″ strips)	BAND B (16″ strips)	BAND C (16″ strips)
Each of 3 dark fabrics	1 @ 3 1/2″ × 18″	1 @ 5 1/2″ × 18″	1 @ 7 1/2″ × 18″
Each of 3 light fabrics	1 @ 7 1/2″ × 18″	1 @ 5 1/2″ × 18″	1 @ 3 1/2″ × 18″

SHOPPING LIST

Each Fabric: 3/8 yard 45″ wide fabric.

Border: For unpieced borders, 1 3/8 yards 45″ wide fabric.
For pieced 4″ borders, 1/2 yard 45″ wide fabric.

Backing: 1 1/2 yards 45″ wide fabric.

Batting: About 38″ × 44″.

Binding: About 4 2/3 yards of 1 1/2″ binding. Can be purchased or cut from 1/4 yard of fabric.

The quilting pattern consists of triangles, but is designed to be quilted in continuous zigzag lines (Fig. 8–4). The long side of the triangle, which I think of as the base of the triangle, is ¼ inch from the seam line, and each end of the long sides is ½ inch in from the end of the rectangle. The third corner, the tip of the triangle, touches one of the base corners of the next triangle in that fabric. Thus the tip is also ¼ inch from the nearby horizontal seam and ½ inch from the nearest vertical seam. Locate the corners of the triangle and use a ruler to mark the sides of the triangle. The quilting line will cross each horizontal seam ¼ inch from the nearest vertical seam.

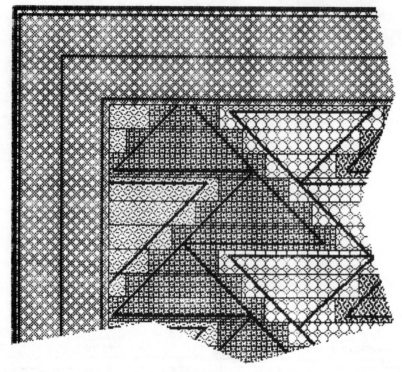

Fig. 8–4. The heavy lines show a quilting pattern for the Ziggurats quilt.

HALF-DROP PATTERNS

When I designed my first multiple-band shift pattern, shown in Fig. 8–5, I intended to piece it as a multiple-band pattern. Then I realized that the segments labeled B and F at the top of the pattern were actually the same except for a shift, as were C and E, and A and G. The labels at the bottom of the pattern show how you can piece the pattern from only four bands by using shifts. You do need to place the edges of the pattern so that what comes off the top goes back on the bottom (the looping principle). The bottom edge of the quilt has been "trimmed," as it must be to take advantage of shifting.

This diamond pattern is one of a large class of patterns called half-drop patterns, which lend themselves naturally to shifted multiple-band piecing. To understand what a half-drop pattern is, first think of a pattern consisting of motifs laid out on a square grid, as in Fig. 8–6. Now imagine that you take alternate columns of motifs and drop them so that the motifs in these columns now lay halfway between the motifs in the other columns, as in Fig. 8–7. This is the meaning of the term *half-drop*. The motifs are really still laid out on a grid, but now it's a diamond-shaped grid, as shown in Fig. 8–8, rather than a rectangular grid. If you look around at fabrics and wallpapers, you'll be amazed at how many half-drop patterns you find.

A B C D E F G F E D C B A B C D E F G F E D C B A

Fig. 8–5. The labels at the top of this pattern show how this quilt could be pieced with segments from seven bands. The labels at the bottom show how, by using shifts, the quilt could be pieced with segments from four bands.

A B C D C B A B C D C B A B C D C B A B C D C B A

Fig. 8–6. In this pattern, elements are arranged in a rectangular grid.

Fig. 8–7. Alternate columns of the original rectangular-grid pattern have been dropped by half an element. The resulting pattern is a half-drop pattern.

Fig. 8–8. Half-drop patterns also can be thought of as being based on a diamond-shaped grid, as shown here.

Center Diamond

Center diamond, shown in Fig. C–9, uses the design shown in Fig. 8–5. (See Table 8–3.) The diamond-shaped grid is obvious in the "paths" between the diamonds. Note, in Fig. 8–9, that the top edge of the quilt falls halfway between grid lines, or ¾ inch from the top grid line. Rectangles at the top of the quilt are ¾, 2¼, or 3¾ inches long. You can avoid these messy measurements by taking advantage of the fact that each loop is cut in the middle of a rectangle. Fold the rectangle to be cut, matching the seams at the ends of the rectangle, and cut along the fold.

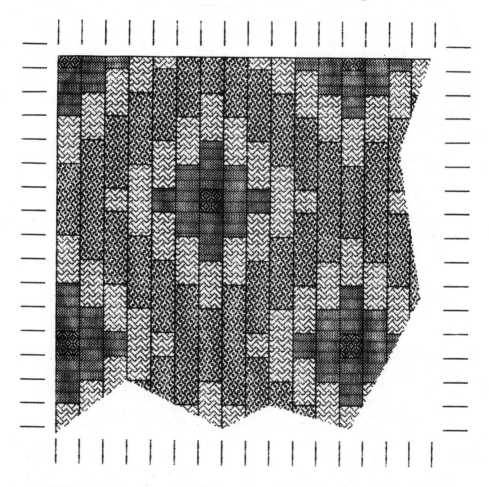

Fig. 8–9. The construction diagram for the Center Diamond quilt includes tick marks for drawing a 1½-inch grid.

Table 8–3. Strips for Center Diamond Quilt.

GRID SIZE: **1 1/2″** Finished Size of Pattern Area: **37 1/2″ × 53 1/2″**

	BAND A (10″ strips)	BAND B (16″ strips)	BAND C (16″ strips)	BAND D (8″ strips)
Background	3 @ 5″ × 10″	3 @ 8″ × 16″	6 @ 5″ × 16″	6 @ 5″ × 8″
Color 1	6 @ 3 1/2″ × 10″	6 @ 3 1/2″ × 16″	6 @ 3 1/2″ × 16″	6 @ 5″ × 8″
			3 @ 2″ × 16″	
Color 2	6 @ 3 1/2″ × 10″	3 @ 5″ × 16″	3 @ 2″ × 16″	
Color 3	3 @ 2″ × 10″			

SHOPPING LIST

Background: 1 3/8 yards 45″ wide fabric.

Color 1: 1 1/4 yards 45″ wide fabric.

Color 2: 1/2 yard 45″ wide fabric.

Color 3: 1/8 yard 45″ wide fabric.

Border: For unpieced borders, 1 7/8 yards 45″ wide fabric.
For pieced 4″ borders, 5/8 yards 45″ wide fabric.

Backing: 2 5/8 yards 45″ wide fabric.

Batting: About 50″ × 66″.

Binding: About 6 yards of 1 1/2″ binding. Can be purchased or cut from 1/4 yard
of fabric.

Figure 8–10 shows the obvious quilting pattern for Center Diamond. On the top edge, the center of the pattern, where the natural turn-around points for the quilting would be, has been taken up in the seam allowance. On the sides of the quilt, the pattern area extends beyond the natural turn-around points. The line that follow the paths between the diamonds cross halfway across the last segment. The lines within the diamonds also could turn around halfway across the last segment, but I think the quilting pattern looks better if they are simply extended to the edge of the pattern area, as shown.

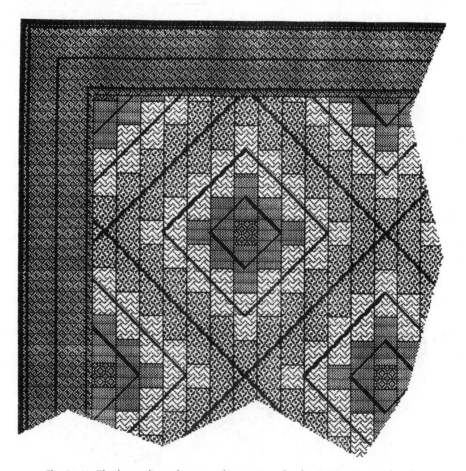

Fig. 8–10. The heavy lines show a quilting pattern for the Center Diamond quilt.

Corner Diamond

Corner Diamond, shown in Fig. 8–11, is clearly related to Center Diamond. The main difference between the two patterns is that Corner Diamond is filled with inverted V shapes, with a single rectangle at the bottom corner of the diamond. A more subtle difference is that the two designs use different numbers of bands. Center Diamond uses four bands, while Corner Diamond uses three (Table 8–4). Although the Corner Diamond uses fewer bands, it uses more colors because each color goes around only two sides of the diamond.

This quilt is a good size for a queen-size bed. The quilting design is much like that for Center Diamond.

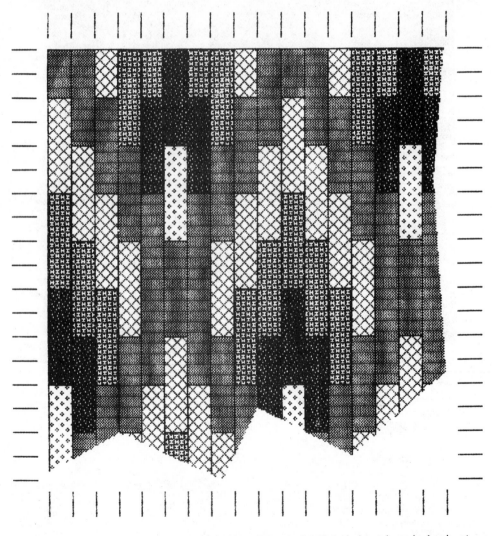

Fig. 8–11. The construction diagram for the Corner Diamond quilt includes tick marks for drawing a 1-inch grid.

Table 8–4. Strips for Corner Diamond Quilt.

GRID SIZE: **1**″ Finished Size of Pattern Area: **61**″ × **79 1/2**″

	BAND A (**19 1/2**″ strips)	BAND B (**36**″ strips)	BAND C (**36**″ strips)
Background	4 @ 4 1/2″ × 19 1/2″	4 @ 8 1/2″ × 36″	8 @ 4 1/2″ × 36″
Color 1	4 @ 4 1/2″ × 19 1/2″	4 @ 4 1/2″ × 36″	8 @ 4 1/2″ × 36″
Color 2	4 @ 4 1/2″ × 19 1/2″	4 @ 4 1/2″ × 36″	4 @ 4 1/2″ × 36″
Color 3	4 @ 4 1/2″ × 19 1/2″	4 @ 4 1/2″ × 36″	
Color 4	4 @ 4 1/2″ × 19 1/2″		

SHOPPING LIST

Background: 2 1/4 yards 45″ wide fabric.

Color 1: 1 7/8 yards 45″ wide fabric.

Color 2: 1 3/8 yards 45″ wide fabric.

Color 3: 7/8 yard 45″ wide fabric.

Color 4: 3/8 yard 45″ wide fabric.

Border: For borders less than about 11″ wide, 3 1/4 yards 45″ wide fabric.

Backing: 6 1/2 yards 45″ wide fabric.

Batting: About 85″ × 114″.

Binding: About 10 3/4 yards of 1 1/2″ binding. Can be purchased or cut from 1/2 yard of fabric.

Heart Throb

Heart throb, shown in Figs. C–15 and C–24, is another half-drop pattern, with a background that suggests the diagonal-grid paths of the Diamond patterns. The pattern uses four bands in an ABCDCBA arrangement (Table 8–5). Band D contains two rectangles in each heart color: one is used as the right edge of the heart to the left of the segment, while the other is the left edge of the heart on the right.

The narrow inner border should be in a contrasting color, probably green, to separate the red border from the pieces of red hearts around the edge of the quilt. The tops of the three center rectangles in the heart fall halfway between the grid lines (Fig. 8–12), so drawing in the grid will be particularly useful for this quilt. Note also that the top and side of the quilt fall halfway between grid lines.

In the Diamond quilts, all segments were the same width, even though as a result the pattern area on the sides of the quilt ran past the natural stopping point, the centerline or mirror line of the pattern. Maintaining the regularity of the segment widths seemed more important than stopping at the mirror lines in those patterns. In Heart Throb, it seemed important for the pattern area to stop at the centers of the hearts. Thus the quilt stops and ends with narrow segments cut 1 inch wide rather

Table 8–5. Strips for Heart Throb Quilt.

GRID SIZE: 1" Finished Size of Pattern Area: **36" × 49 1/2"**

	BAND A (9 1/2" strips)	BAND B (18" strips)	BAND C (18" strips)	BAND D (9" strips)
Background	5 @ 5" × 9 1/2"	5 @ 5" × 18"	5 @ 5 1/2" × 18"	10 @ 2 1/2" × 9"
Each of 5 red fabrics	1 @ 6" × 9 1/2"	1 @ 6" × 18"	1 @ 5 1/2" × 18"	2 @ 3 1/2" × 9"

SHOPPING LIST

Background: 1 1/8 yards 45" wide fabric.
Each red: 3/8 yard 45" wide fabric.
Inner border: 1/4 yard 45" wide fabric.
Border: For unpieced borders, 1 3/4 yards 45" wide fabric.
For pieced 4" borders, 5/8 yards 45" wide fabric.
Backing: If border is less than about 4" wide, backing can be unpieced, will require 1 3/4 yards 45" wide fabric.
If border is wider, backing will be pieced, will require 2 3/4 yards 45" wide fabric.
Batting: About 48" × 62".
Binding: About 5 3/4 yards of 1 1/2" binding. Can be purchased or cut from 1/4 yard of fabric.

than 1½ inches wide. To accommodate these narrow strips, you can make a couple of special 1-inch marks on the paper template marked every 1½ inches, or you can make a special paper template marked as follows:

1, 2½, 4, 5½, 10 (center segment of first complete heart),
11½, 13, 14½, 16, 17½, 19 (center segment of second heart),
20½, 22, 23½, 25, 26½, 28 (center segment of central heart),
29½, 31, 32½, 34, 35½, 37 (center segment of fourth heart),
38½, 40, 41½, 43, 44½, 46 (center segment of last complete heart),
47½, 49, 50½, 52, 53½, 54½

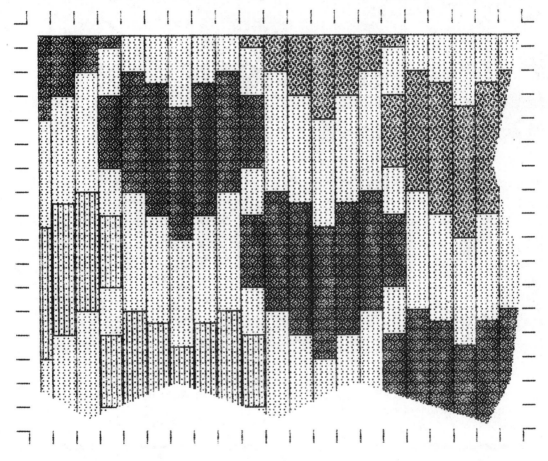

Fig. 8–12. The construction diagram for the Heart Throb quilt includes tick marks for making a 1-inch grid.

To mark the diamond lattice in the quilting pattern (Fig. 8–13) find the key points located just above the edges of the hearts. The quilted hearts reinforce the heart idea, and make the rather crude pieced heart look more heart-like. Trace the pattern in Fig. 8–14, glue it to cardboard, and cut out the heart-shaped cardboard template.

Fig. 8–13. The heavy lines show a quilting pattern for the Heart Throb quilt. The lattice lines are drawn by first locating the key points, one of which is circled.

Fig. 8 – 14. This is a full-sized pattern for the heart shape used in the quilting of the Heart Throb quilt.

Peacock Eyes

You can vary multiple-band shift patterns, like any others, by using strips of different widths. Peacock Eyes, shown in Figs. C–12, C–21, and 8–15), is such a variation on corner diamond. It is based on a type of needlepoint pattern that, although not composed of unbroken rows of color like the "pure" bargello patterns, generally appears in books on bargello. Once again, the pattern has been stripped down to essentials so that it is on a reasonable scale for piecing.

In my quilt, I used a gold mylar fabric for the centers of the eyes. It tended to ravel, so I had to reinforce it with fusable interfacing, but it added a lot of punch to the quilt. Whatever fabric you use for this element in the design should be a dramatic one. (See Table 8–6.)

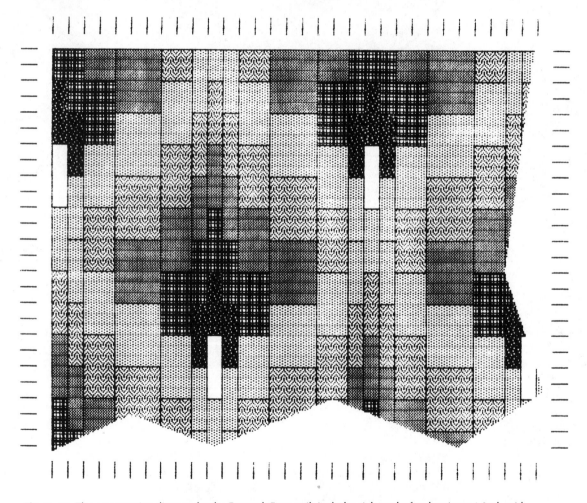

Fig. 8–15. The construction diagram for the Peacock Eyes quilt includes tick marks for drawing a 1-inch grid.

Table 8–6. Strips for Peacock Eyes Quilt.

GRID SIZE: 1" Finished Size of Pattern Area: **61" × 71 1/2"**

	BAND A (**10 1/2" strips**)	BAND B (**18" strips**)	BAND C (**30" strips**)	BAND D (**21" strips**)
Background	3 @ 4 1/2" × 10 1/2"	6 @ 4 1/2" × 18"	6 @ 4 1/2" × 30"	6 @ 4 1/2" × 21"
Color 1:	3 @ 4 1/2" × 10 1/2"	3 @ 4 1/2" × 18"	6 @ 4 1/2" × 30"	6 @ 4 1/2" × 21"
Color 2:	3 @ 4 1/2" × 10 1/2"	3 @ 4 1/2" × 18"	3 @ 4 1/2" × 30"	6 @ 4 1/2" × 21"
Color 3:	3 @ 4 1/2" × 10 1/2"	3 @ 4 1/2" × 18"	3 @ 4 1/2" × 30"	
Color 4:	3 @ 4 1/2" × 10 1/2"	3 @ 4 1/2" × 18"		
Color 5:	3 @ 4 1/2" × 10 1/2"			

SHOPPING LIST

Background:	1 5/8 yards 45" wide fabric.
Color 1:	1 1/2 yards 45" wide fabric.
Color 2:	1 1/8 yards 45" wide fabric.
Color 3:	3/4 yard 45" wide fabric.
Color 4:	1/2 yard 45" wide fabric.
Color 5:	1/4 yard 45" wide fabric.
Border:	For borders less than about 11" wide, 2 5/8 yards 45" wide fabric.
Backing:	5 1/2 yards 45" wide fabric.
Batting:	About 85" × 96".
Binding:	About 9 3/4 yards of 1 1/2" binding. Can be purchased or cut from 3/8 yard of fabric.

The quilt requires a special paper template. You can make a full-length template marked as follows, or you can make a half-length template 41 inches long. If you use a half-length template, make each strip in two pieces. Mark the first piece of the strip to 41 inches, according to the template. For the second piece of the strip, start at the second cross-cut line (the 1½ inch mark, rather than the zero mark), and mark from that point through to the 41-inch mark.

1½, 3, 5½ 9, 11½, 13, 15 (center of first "eye"),
16½, 19, 22½, 25, 26½, 28 (center of second "eye"),
29½, 32, 35½, 38, 39½, 41 (center of third "eye"),
42½, 45, 48½, 51, 52½, 54 (center of fourth "eye"),
55½, 58, 61½, 64, 65½, 67 (center of fifth "eye"),
68½, 71, 74½, 77, 78½, 90

The addition of quilting made a huge difference to this quilt (Fig. 8–16). The curves that were suggested, rather weakly, by the piecing, are very strong in the quilting. This is a quilt that "demanded" quilting from me. I first quilted the lines that run within each color as well as one line up each path. The quilt seemed limp, so I added the additional quilting, which made the quilt come alive.

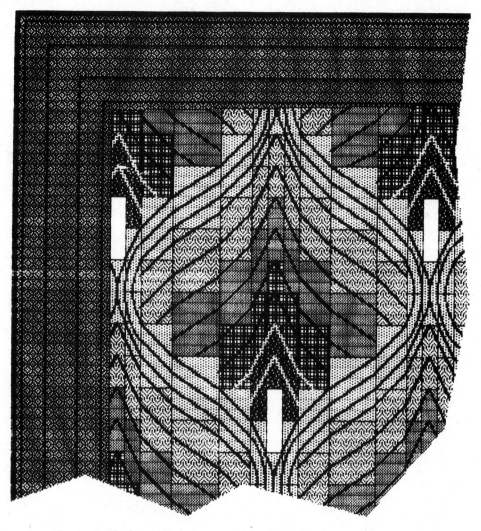

Fig. 8 – 16. The heavy lines show a quilting design for the Peacock Eyes quilt.

Orchard

Figure 8–17 shows how varying offsets can be used to achieve curves. I call this pattern Orchard, since the motifs look like little trees lined up in neat rows. (See Table 8–7.)

As you can see from Fig. 8–18, the spacing of rectangles in this quilt is a bit tricky. The offsets between segments can best be followed by looking at the background rectangles, starting with the one above the center of a tree. The offsets are 1 inch, 2 inches, 2½ inches, and 3½ inches. Because of the way the rows of trees are packed together, the 1-inch offset at the top of a tree, which corresponds to a 3½-inch overlap between rectangles of the same fabric, is on the same seam as the 3½-inch offset at the bottom of the tree, next to the tree "trunk." In the same way, the 2-inch and the 2½-inch offsets share the same seams.

Figure 8–19 shows a quilting pattern for Orchard. Within the trees, lines of quilting run within each color and along joins between colors. The quilting of the background parallels the line of quilting at the tops of the trees. Draw the quilting pattern in the usual way, by marking the midpoints of overlaps between rectangles.

Table 8–7. Strips for Orchard Quilt.

GRID SIZE: **1 1/2"** Finished Size of Pattern Area: **61 1/2" × 80 1/2"**

	BAND A (22" strips)	BAND B (40" strips)	BAND C (40" strips)
Background	6 @ 5" × 22"	6 @ 5" × 45"	6 @ 5" × 45"
Color 1 (top color)	3 @ 5" × 22"	6 @ 5" × 45"	6 @ 5" × 45"
Color 2	3 @ 5" × 22"	3 @ 5" × 45"	6 @ 5" × 45"
Color 3	3 @ 5" × 22"	3 @ 5" × 45"	
Color 4 (trunk color)	3 @ 5" × 22"		

SHOPPING LIST
- Background: 1 3/4 yards 45" wide fabric.
- Color 1: 1 3/8 yards 45" wide fabric.
- Color 2: 1 1/4 yards 45" wide fabric.
- Color 3: 3/4 yard 45" wide fabric.
- Color 4: 3/8 yard 45" wide fabric.
- Inner Border: 3/8 yard 45" wide fabric.
- Border: If less than about 11" wide, 2 5/8 yards 45" wide fabric.
- Backing: 5 1/4 yards 45" wide fabric.
- Batting: About 85" × 95".
- Binding: About 9 3/4 yards of 1 1/2" binding. Can be purchased or cut from 3/8 yard of fabric.

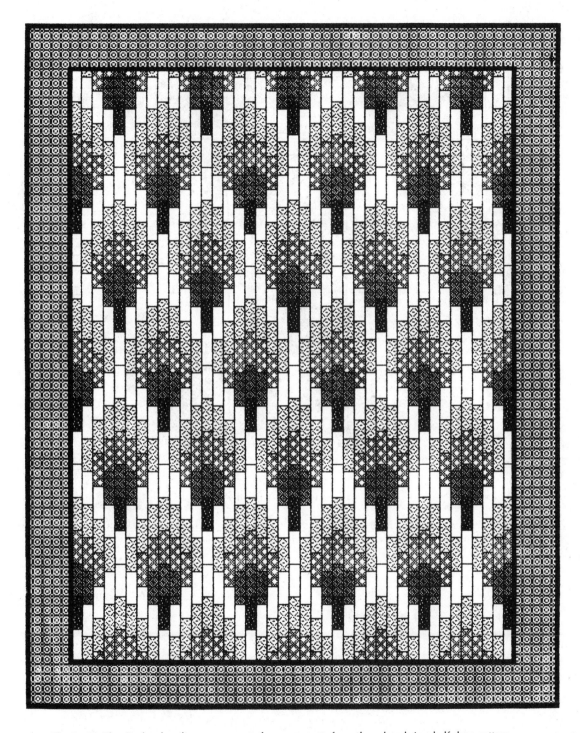

Fig. 8–17. The Orchard quilt uses segments from segments from three bands in a half-drop pattern.

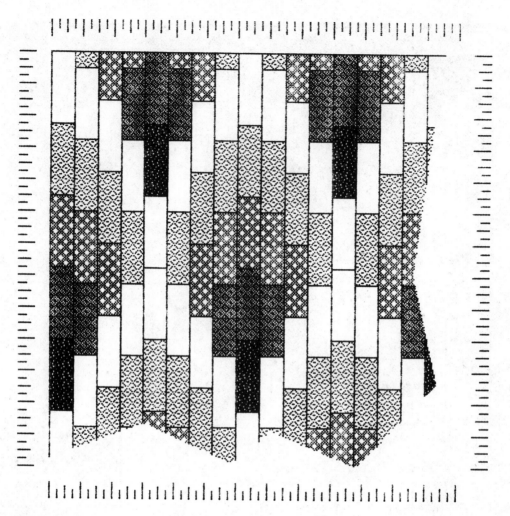

Fig. 8–18. The construction diagram for the Orchard quilt includes tick marks for drawing a 1½-inch grid. The same diagram is used for the Autumn Orchard quilt, which uses a ¾-inch grid.

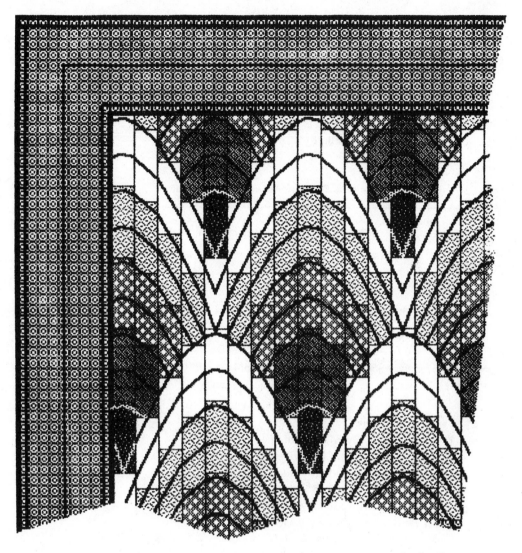

Fig. 8 – 19. The heavy lines show a quilting design for the Orchard quilt.

Autumn Orchard

The Autumn Orchard quilt, based on the Orchard pattern, is shown in Figs. C–16 and C–23. It uses 25 fabrics (Table 8–8), rather than the five fabrics of Orchard. Each type of tree appears in a row with half-trees on the ends and in a row without half trees. The background fabric is different for each row of trees, as well.

The grid for Autumn Orchard is ¾ inch, half the size of the grid for the Orchard quilt. Because of this, the quilting is simpler. Only the quilting lines that fall within each color are retained. (See Fig. 8–20.)

Table 8–8. Strips for Autumn Orchard Quilt.

GRID SIZE: **3/4"** Size of Finished Pattern Area: **54 3/4" × 67"**

	BAND A (23 3/4" strips)	BAND B (45" strips)	BAND C (22 1/2" strips)
Each of 5 backgrounds	2 @ 2 3/4" × 22 1/2"	2 @ 2 3/4" × 40"	2 @ 2 3/4" × 40"
Each of 5 top colors	1 @ 2 3/4" × 22 1/2"	2 @ 2 3/4" × 40"	2 @ 2 3/4" × 40"
Each of 5 2nd colors	1 @ 2 3/4" × 22 1/2"	1 @ 2 3/4" × 40"	2 @ 2 3/4" × 40"
Each of 5 3rd colors	1 @ 2 3/4" × 22 1/2"	1 @ 2 3/4" × 40"	
Each of 5 trunk colors	1 @ 2 3/4" × 22 1/2"		

SHOPPING LIST

Each background: 1/2 yard 45" wide fabric.

Each top color: 3/8 yard 45" wide fabric.

Each second color: 1/4 yard 45" wide fabric.

Each third color: 1/4 yard 45" wide fabric.

Each trunk color: 1/8 yard 45" wide fabric.

Inner Border: 3/8 yard 45" wide fabric.

Border: If less than about 11" wide, 2 1/2 yards 45" wide fabric.

Backing: 4 1/4 yards 45" wide fabric.

Batting: About 79" × 91".

Binding: About 9 yards of 1 1/2" binding. Can be purchased or cut from 3/8 yard of fabric.

Fig. 8 – 20. The heavy lines show a quilting design for the Autumn Orchard quilt. Because this quilt is based on a smaller grid, a less elaborate quilting pattern than that used for the Orchard quilt can be used.

Spring Tender

Spring Tender gives some final twists to the half-drop pattern idea (Table 8–9 and Fig. C–17). This complicated-looking pattern is really a center diamond variation. Figure 8–21 shows the basic center diamond, which does not actually appear in the quilt, along with two distorted diamonds made from the same group of rectangles. The first I call a *kite*, and the second a *lozenge*. You can think of these shapes as the result of pushing the diamond out of shape. The diamonds are linked together: the square that finishes one diamond also starts the next (Fig. 8–22.) Therefore, the background is cut into separate zigzagging bands.

The quilting in the background zigzags always crosses the seam lines halfway along the overlap between two segments (Fig. 8–23). Note that although most of the rectangles in the background are 1 × 5 units, those at the bends are only 4 units high. The quilting of the outer ring is also not too difficult to mark. The rectangles at the sides and the top and bottom of the ring are all 1-×-5 units. The quilting lines link the centers of these rectangles.

For the quilting of the inner rings, mark the centers of the side rectangles, which are 1 × 7 units. Then mark the midpoints of the overlaps with the top and bottom rectangles and connect the centers and the midpoints. These lines meet in the top and bottom rectangles, but not in the centers of those rectangles.

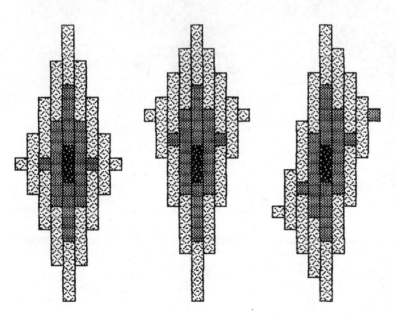

Fig. 8–21. The center diamond (left) is the basis of the kite (center) and the lozenge (right) in the Spring Tender quilt.

Table 8-9. Strips for Spring Tender Quilt.

GRID SIZE: **1"** Size of Finished Pattern Area: **73" × 95 1/2"**

	BAND A (28 1/2" strips)	BAND B (54" strips)	BAND C (27" strips)
Each of 3 backgrounds:	2 @ 4 1/2" × 28 1/2"	2 @ 5 1/2" × 54"	2 @ 5 1/2" × 27"
Each of 3 lights:) (outer rings)	2 @ 5 1/2" × 28 1/2" 1 @ 1 1/2" × 28 1/2"	3 @ 5 1/2" × 54"	4 @ 5 1/2" × 27"
Each of 3 mediums: (inner rings)	2 @ 5 1/2" × 28 1/2"	1 @ 7 1/2" × 54"	2 @ 1 1/2" × 27"
Each of 3 darks: (centers)	1 @ 3 1/2" × 28 1/2"		

SHOPPING LIST

Each background fabric: 1 yard 45" wide fabric.

Each light fabric: 1 3/8 yards 45" wide fabric.

Each medium fabric: 1/2 yard 45" wide fabric.

Each dark fabric: 1/8 yard 45" wide fabric.

Border: For borders up to about 10" wide, 3 1/4 yards 45" wide fabric.

Backing: For backing pieced from three horizontal strips, 8 yards 45" wide fabric.

Batting: Exact size depends on border width, but about 100" × 120".

Binding: About 11 3/4 yards of 1 1/2" binding. Can be purchased or cut from 1/2 yard of fabric.

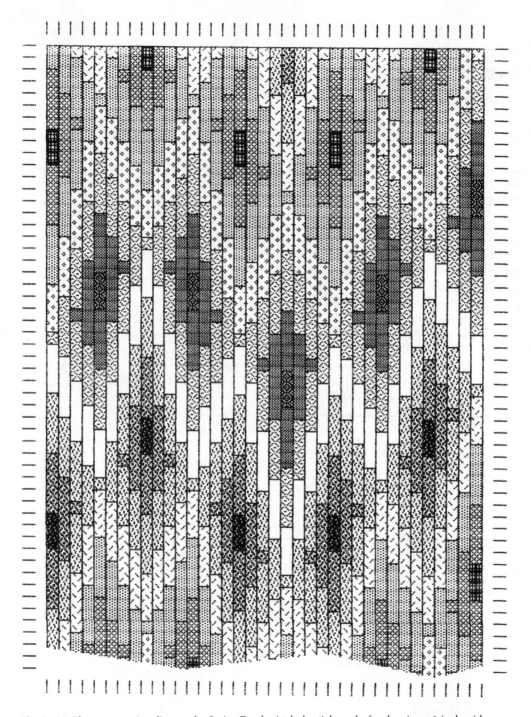

Fig. 8–22. The construction diagram for Spring Tender includes tick marks for drawing a 1-inch grid.

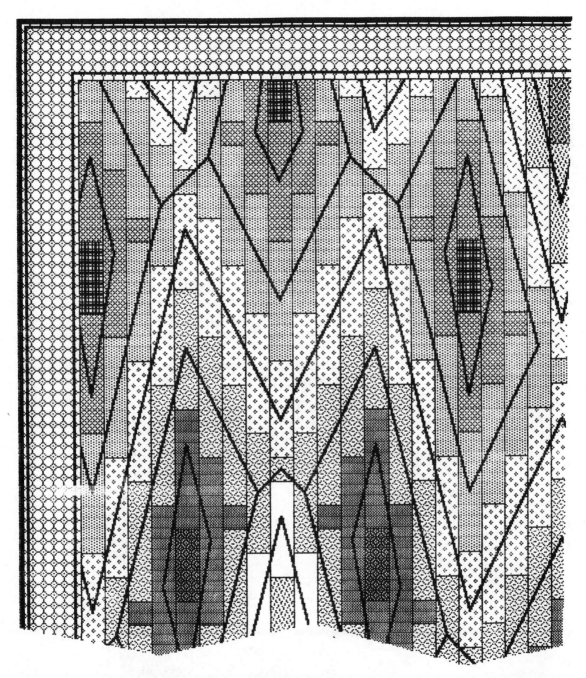

Fig. 8–23. The heavy lines show the quilting pattern for the Spring Tender. The lines of quilting follow the colors in the usual way. Where a color "spikes," the quilting also spikes.

HUNGARIAN POINT

Hungarian Point is the name of a type of needlepoint closely related to bargello, but composed of short and long stitches. Hungarian Point, like bargello, can be worked by laying out a foundation row in one color, then building successive rows of other colors. The long and short stitches in one row are offset from those in other rows, as shown in Fig. 8 – 24, so that, in the long run, each column of stitches has the same number of long and short stitches. The places where the design reverses direction make Hungarian Point designs exciting, creating wonderful spiky shapes, which remind many people of skylines or spires.

Figure 8 – 25 shows three colorings of a Hungarian Point pattern made by sewing three short stitches and one long stitch. Examine a vertical stack of stitches, the part that would become a segment in the quilt. Here too, there are three short stitches and one long one. In the second coloring, with four colors, the long rectangle in each stack or segment is always the same color. The quilt would be made of four types of segments, each with the long stitch in one of the four colors.

The first coloring uses three colors and the long-and-short pattern of the segment does not match up with the color pattern. However, if you look at the long stack of 12 rectangles indicated by the arrows, you'll see that there is, finally, a repeat in the pattern. Examine other parts of the pattern, and you'll see that, in fact, all the stacks contain this same sequence of 12 stitches, so that a quilt in this pattern would be made with one type of segment.

Fig. 8 – 24. In this simple example of Hungarian Point needlepoint, a cycle of three short stitches and one long stitch is used for every color.

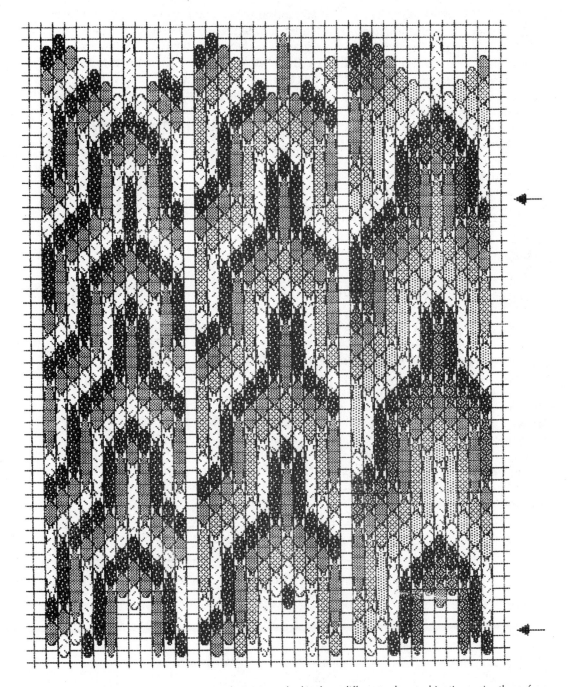

Fig. 8–25. A portion of one Hungarian Point design is worked in three different color combinations using three, four, and six colors.

The last coloring uses six colors. Examination of the color-and-shape pattern shows that, in any stack, the pattern repeats after 12 stitches. However, comparison of stacks shows that there are two types of stacks, which alternate. Three colors show up as long stitches in one type of stack, while the other three colors show up as long stitches in the other type of stack. Thus, this quilt would be made from two bands.

You can see that the number of colors you use to create a quilt in a Hungarian Point design determines the number of bands needed. The pattern looks subtly different with different numbers of colors; different colors are emphasized by their appearance in the dramatic "spike" positions in the design.

Because the number of colors determines the length of the vertical repeat, it will determine the possible heights of the pattern area. In order to take advantage of shifting, what goes off the top must come back at the bottom (the looping principle). So, for instance, the four-color variation could be used for a quilt 16 stitches tall, but the others, since they repeat in 12 stitches, could not.

Standing Wave

Standing Wave, named for its combination of a wave form and a feeling of stability, is shown in Figs. 8–26, C–13, and C–22. It was designed in collaboration with my aunt, Naoma O'Neill, who made a slightly different quilt in the same pattern. This pattern uses four shorts and a long, and a sequence of six colors (Table 8–10). Cover up most of Fig. 8–26 and look at one segment. Note that each color appears once as a wide strip and four times as a narrow strip. Regardless of size, the colors always appear in the same order within the band.

If you compare the quilt in Fig. 8–26 with Naoma's original quilt, you'll see that the main difference is that Naoma's quilt is somewhat larger. The longer quilt cannot be made with only one band. To make the longer quilt, make six different bands and construct the quilt strictly as a multiple-band pattern. The Standing Wave pattern appears in this chapter on multiple-band shift patterns because, in a way, it is a hybrid. As shown in Fig. 8–26, it is constructed from one band using shifts only, while Naoma's Standing Wave was constructed from six bands, without any shifts. (See Figs. 8–27 and 8–28.)

Table 8–10. Strips for Standing Wave Quilt.

GRID SIZE: " Size of Finished Pattern Area: **61" × 83 1/2"**

Each of 6 colors: 4 @ 2 1/2" × 91 1/2" 1 @ 6 1/2" × 91 1/2"

SHOPPING LIST
Each fabric: 1 1/8 yard 45" wide fabric.
   Border: For pieced 1" wide border, 3/8 yard 45" wide fabric.
   Backing: 3 3/4 yards 45" wide fabric.
   Batting: About 67" × 89".
   Binding: About 8 1/3 yards of 1 1/2" binding. Can be purchased or cut from 3/8 yard of fabric.

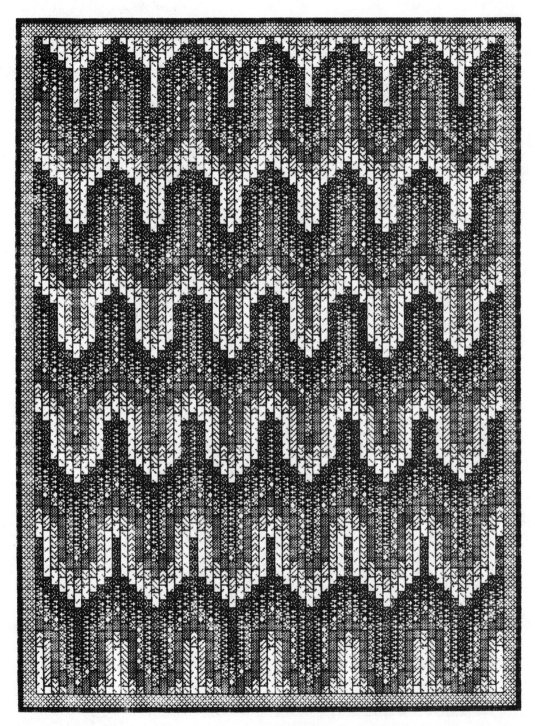

Fig. 8–26. The Standing Wave quilt uses a Hungarian Point pattern with four narrow strips and one wide strip in each color. The version shown is actually a one-band pattern.

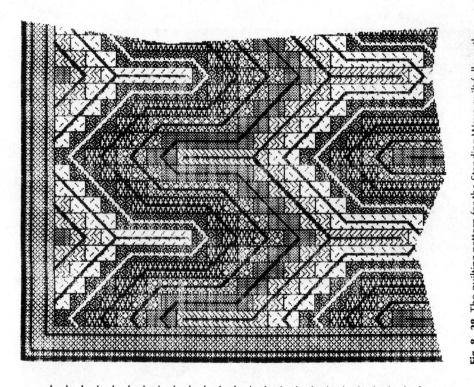

Fig. 8–28. The quilting pattern for the Standing Wave quilt follows the colors in the usual way. Where a color spikes, the quilting line also spikes. Quilt down the spike to a point ½ inch from the end of the rectangle.

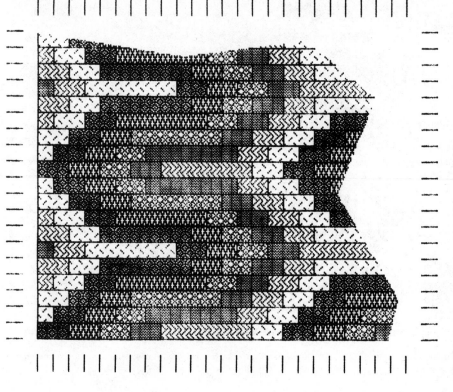

Fig. 8–27. The construction diagram for the Standing Wave quilt includes tick marks for drawing a 1-inch grid.

156

Hungarian Spires

Hungarian Spires uses two short and two long stitches and 10 colors (Table 8–11). The pattern repeats every 20 rectangles and requires two bands. With 10 colors, you can do quite a bit with shading and contrast between colors. The most dramatic part of the color combination shown is in the area surrounding the white rows, which were placed so that they would be nearly unbroken. The white row does not cross the top-to-bottom break except at the very edges of the quilt (Fig. 8–29). Quilting is similar to that for Standing Wave.

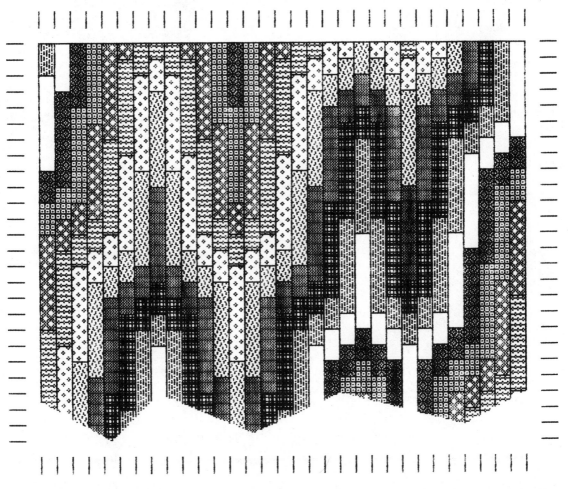

Fig. 8–29. The construction diagram for the Hungarian Spires quilt includes tick marks for drawing a 1-inch grid.

Table 8 – 11. Strips for Hungarian Spires Quilt.

GRID SIZE: **1″** Size of Finished Pattern Area: **61″ × 79 1/2″**

	BAND A **(46 1/2″ strips)**	BAND B **(45″ strips)**
Each of 10 colors:	1 @ 2 1/2″ × 46 1/2″	1 @ 2 1/2″ × 45″
	1 @ 6 1/2″ × 46 1/2″	1 @ 6 1/2″ × 45″

SHOPPING LIST

Each fabric: 5/8 yard 45″ wide fabric.

Inner Border: 1/4 yard 45″ wide fabric.

Border: For borders less than about 11″, 2 7/8 yards 45″ wide fabric.

Backing: 5 3/4 yards 45″ wide fabric.

Batting: About 85″ × 104″.

Binding: About 10 1/4 yards of 1 1/2″ binding. Can be purchased or cut from 1/2 yard of fabric.

Chapter 9
Designing Your Own Quilts

It can be a long jump from following the prepared tables and diagrams for the projects in this book to preparing a pattern of your own. This chapter includes instructions for doing all the bookkeeping necessary to prepare your own tables and diagrams and to calculate yardages, either for modified versions of projects in this book or for completely new projects. Also included are suggestions on how to adapt patterns from other sources, as well as methods you can use to create original designs.

RESIZING

You might want to change the size of a project in this book in one of two basic ways. You might want to keep the proportions of the original, but make it smaller or larger overall by changing the grid size. Instead, you may want to stay at the same scale, but change the proportions of the original, making it a bit longer, shorter, wider, or narrower. Of course, you might want to change both grid size and proportions, in which case you can simply make one change followed by the other.

Changing Grid Size

I made the Striped Sampler as a wall hanging by using a ½-inch grid rather than a 1-inch grid. You might guess that the strips for the new quilt would be half as wide as those for the larger quilt. However, the seam allowances are always ¼ inch wide, so they don't vary with the grid. The key to recalculating strip widths is to think in terms of the finished width of a strip, which is always ½ inch less than the cut width. Table 9–1 shows how the widths for the smaller Striped Sampler were calculated.

The process for recalculating the length of a strip is similar. Part of the length of the strip makes up the pattern area and part is needed for seam allowances. For patterns composed of segments of a single width, this is not too difficult. Figure out the number of segments that will be cut from a strip, either by counting them in the diagram or by dividing the original length of the strip by the original cut width of the segment. Multiply the number of segments by the new cut width of the segment to get the new length of the strip. These calculations are shown in Table 9–2.

To make a new table for the wall-hanging Striped Sampler, I made a copy of the original table and, using Table 9–1 and a red pen, 1 crossed off the original strip widths and wrote in the new strip widths. For the strip lengths, I went through a similar process, using Table 9–2. This conversion was fast, since there were only three strip lengths and all the strips of the same length were in the same column of the table.

When the segments in a pattern are of different widths, I use a different method to calculate the new strip lengths. The total length of the strip is composed of the length needed for the pattern and the length needed for the seam allowances. Every segment has two quarter-inch seam allowances, so the total length needed for seam allowances is 1½ inch times the number of segments. You can simply count the segments in the diagram, regardless of size, and multiply by ½ inch. The rest of the strip is the length needed for the pattern, and is the part that is proportional to the grid size. Table 9–3 shows how to resize the Gentle Rainbow quilt from a 1-inch grid to a 1½-inch grid.

So, that's how to resize a quilt. If you're intimidated by numbers, buy yourself a simple calculator and do all the arithmetic twice or three times just to reassure yourself that it's right. Even more important is to write your calculations down in an organized way, in little tables like those shown in this book. If you write it down, you're likely to notice obvious errors and less likely to leave out important pieces.

Changing a Quilt's Proportions

The method for adjusting the length of a project is a little different from the method for adjusting the width of a project. For the purposes of this section, we'll assume that the project you want to adjust is one in which the segments are vertical. If you want to adjust one of the projects with horizontal strips, turn the diagram sideways, and interchange "length" and "width" in your thinking.

Changing a Quilt's Width. It's almost always simplest to adjust the width of a pattern by adding or subtracting segments. Many patterns have a definite repeat, in which case you'll probably want to add or delete a complete block of segments. Adjusting a pattern by stretching or squashing the whole pattern horizontally will change the proportions of the pattern and usually leads to a lot of messy arithmetic.

The changes to the tables are fairly simple, since only the strip lengths will need to change. suppose, for example, that you're making the Corner Diamond quilt, but you want it to fit the top of a double bed, rather than a queen-size bed. The pattern area given is 61 inches wide, while a double bed is 54 inches wide. The pattern has a definite 10-inch repeat, so you decide to leave off one repeat and make a pattern area 51 inches wide, which, perhaps with an inner border, is close to the 54 inches desired. Removing one repeat from the Corner Diamond pattern means taking off two A segments, four B segments, and four C segments. The modifications to the strip lengths for Bands A, B, and C are shown in Table 9–4.

Changing a Quilt's Length. In some shift patterns, like Shazam or The Vaults, each strip is more or less independent, so you can adjust the length of the quilt by adding or deleting strips at will. At the other extreme, the lengths of the Hungarian point patterns are intimately related to the pattern and the number of colors used. For most other quilts, you'll want to adjust the length in one-repeat increments.

160

Table 9–1. Resizing Striped Sampler: Strip Widths.

STRIPS FOR ORIGINAL QUILT		STRIPS FOR SMALLER QUILT	
Cut	Finished	Finished	Cut
1 1/2 "	1 "	1/2 "	1 "
2 1/2 "	2 "	1 "	1 1/2 "
3 1/2 "	3 "	1 1/2 "	2 "
4 1/2 "	4 "	2 "	2 1/2 "
5 1/2 "	5 "	2 1/2 "	3 "

Table 9–2. Resizing Striped Sampler: Strip Lengths.

STRIPS FOR ORIGINAL QUILT				STRIPS FOR SMALLER QUILT		
Number of Segments	Strip Cut Length	Segment Cut Width	Segment Finished Width	Segment Finished Width	Segment Cut Width	Strip Cut Length
8	12 "	1 1/2 "	1 "	1/2 "	1 "	8 "
14	21 "	1 1/2 "	1 "	1/2 "	1 "	14 "
7	10 1/2 "	1 1/2 "	1 "	1/2 "	1 "	7 "

Table 9–3. Resizing Gentle Rainbow: Strip Lengths.

STRIPS FOR ORIGINAL QUILT				STRIPS FOR SMALLER QUILT		
Number of Segments	Strip Cut Length	Strip Cut Length	Length For S.A.'s	Length For Pattern	Length For Pattern	Length For S.A.'s
23	46 1/2 "	11 1/2 "	35 "	17 1/2 "	11 1/2 "	29 "

Table 9–4. Adjusting Width of Corner Diamond Quilt.

	STRIPS FOR ORIGINAL QUILT			STRIPS FOR SMALLER QUILT		
Band	Strip Cut Length	Number of Segments	Segment Finished Width	Segment Finished Width	Number of Segments	Strip Cut Length
A	19 1/2 "	13	1 1/2 "	1 1/2 "	11	16 1/2 "
B	36 "	24	1 1/2 "	1 1/2 "	20	30 "
C	36 "	24	1 1/2 "	1 1/2 "	20	30 "

Let's return to the Corner Diamond, which we were adjusting to fit a double bed. This is a shift pattern, so the off-at-the-bottom, on-at-the-top rule needs to be observed. A complete repeat is five strips, or 20 inches, long. The original 80 inches is a bit longer than the top of the usual 75-inch double bed, but 60 inches is much shorter.

Let's stop to think about how a quilt actually will fit on a bed. At the head of the bed, the border does not hang off the bed, so we have a bit extra. However, the pillows usually take up some of the length, unless they're placed on top of the quilt. Many people actually use quite a bit of length by putting a fold under the edge of the pillow.

If I were planning a moderate border on the Corner Diamond Quilt and wanted the pattern area to cover the pillows, I'd go ahead with the full 80 inches of the original quilt. In other circumstances, however, I'd go for 60 inches. I might put a wide border on the quilt, say 20 inches, and cover the pillows with this border. I might put a 6-inch border on the quilt, use it on top of a solid-color bedspread, and simply tuck the top border of the quilt under the pillows in the fold of the bedspread. I might make the bed with fancy sheets and pillowcases which the quilt would purposely leave uncovered.

To make a shorter version of the Corner Diamond quilt, figure out how many strips of each color go into one repeat, and delete those. The original quilt had 4 repeats, which we're proposing to cut back to 3. If you look back at Table 8–4, you'll see that, in most cases, the number of strips needed of any particular color is given as 4. Simply change these 4s to 3s. In Band C, there are two colors for which 8 strips are needed. One-fourth of these strips would also be deleted, so the 8s would be changed to 6s.

PREPARING A TABLE FOR A NEW PATTERN

Preparing a new table simply means counting segments and strips, adding in the right amounts for seam allowances, and writing it all down in tabular form. The form of the table, although it might seem imposing, actually makes it easier to keep track of how many strips of which sizes you need. You might find that it's easier to write neat tables on graph paper.

Suppose you worked up the diagram shown in Fig. 9–1 and decided on a grid size of 1 inch. First, label the segments as shown at the bottom of the diagram. Then count the segments in each band and determine the length of the strips for each band, as shown in Table 9–5.

This part of the process would be more complicated for a quilt with segments of varying widths. For such a quilt, you'd need to count the number of segments of each width, multiply each count by the appropriate cut width of a segment, and add all the products to get the total length of the strip. I double-check these more complicated calculations by making up the paper template and checking to see that the length of the template is the same as the length I've calculated for the strips.

Table 9–5. New Quilt: Strip Lengths.

Band	Number of Segments	Segment Cut Width	Strip Cut Length
A	7	1 1/2"	10 1/2
B	12	1 1/2"	18"
C	6	1 1/2"	9"

Fig. 9 – 1. This working drawing for a Center Diamond pattern is labeled with segment types at the bottom.

A B C B A B C B A B C B A B C B A B C B A B C B A

The next step in the process of making a table is to count the number of strips of each width and color needed for each band. You can tally them by moving down a segment in your diagram, checking the strips off as you go. If the pattern uses shifts, remember that the rectangles at the top and the bottom of the diagram might be pieces of larger rectangles that were cut in the looping process.

In our example, the top rectangle in each segment of the diagram does in fact go together with the bottom rectangle in the segment to make a larger rectangle. Tallies of rectangles in a strip from Band A are shown in Table 9 – 6. The finished height is used in the tally because that's what shows up in the diagram; we'll worry about adding seam allowances in the next step.

The *Total* line in this table is a double check, to be sure we haven't left out any strips. Go back to the diagram and figure the height of the band to be sure that it matches this total.

Table 9–6. Band A of New Quilt: Preliminary Table for Strip Widths.

Fabric	Number of Rectangles	Rectangle Finished Height	Total Height
Background	3	3″	9″
Dark 1	2	2″	4″
Dark 2	2	2″	4″
Dark 3	2	2″	4″
Light 1	1	3″	3″
Light 2	1	3″	3″
Light 3	1	3″	3″
Total			30″

The preliminary table for Band C is similar to that for Band A and is not shown. The one for Band B (Table 9–7) however, is slightly different, since there are, for some fabrics, strips of more than one width. Simply include a line in the table for each rectangle height.

Table 9–8 shows the finished table for the new quilt. The table looks a lot shorter than Tables 9–6 and 9–7 because I've grouped all the darks and all the lights together. I've used this method because each of the darks needs exactly the same complement of strips; you could keep each dark and each light separate if it seemed clearer to you. Another way in which Table 9–8 is compressed is that each place in the table actually contains three pieces of information: the number of strips, their width, and their length. The number of strips is the same as the *Number of Rectangles* in Table 9–8 or 9–10. The width of the strip is ½ inch more than the corresponding measurement in the *Rectangle Finished Height* column of Table 9–8 or 9–9, since it incorparates the two quarter-inch seam allowances. The strip length, which is the same for all items in a column, also has been written under the name of the band at the head of the column.

FIGURING YARDAGE

Calculating yardage is a worry for many quilters, caused, I think, by two conflicting fears: fear of running out of fabric and fear of wasting money by buying too much fabric. Personally, I've decided that buying extra fabric is not a waste because sooner or later I'll use it in another quilt. Only with very expensive fabric do I agonize over buying an extra quarter yard. Of course, I have to admit that I'm a professional quilter, and my quilting pays for itself, so buying fabric is easy to justify. Still, I think that, for most people, the fear of running out of fabric is the stronger fear, so I tend to be generous in calculating yardages.

When preparing a shopping list, I assume that I'll be getting standard 45-inch-wide fabric, which is usually a little narrower than 45 inches after it's been washed and had the selvages trimmed off. If I find a wider fabric, I usually go ahead and get the amount I calculated for my shopping list, knowing I'll have fabric left over. With narrower fabric, or with expensive wide fabric, I do a quick recalculation in the store.

Table 9–7. Band B of New Quilt: Preliminary Table for Strip Widths.

Fabric	Number of Rectangles	Rectangle Finished Height	Total Height
Background	6	2″	12″
Dark 1	2	2″	4″
	1	1″	1″
Dark 2	2	2″	4″
	1	1″	1″
Dark 3	2	2″	4″
	1	1″	1″
Light 1	1	1″	1″
Light 2	1	1″	1″
Light 3	1	1″	1″
Total			30″

Table 9–8. Strips for New Quilt.

Grid Size: **1″** Finished Size of Pattern Area: **25″ × 29 1/2″**

	Band A **(10 1/2″ strips)**	Band B **(18″ strips)**	Band C **(9″ strips)**
Background	3 @ 3 1/2″ × 10 1/2″	6 @ 2 1/2″ × 18″	6 @ 2 1/2″ × 9″
Each of 3 Darks	2 @ 2 1/2″ × 10 1/2″	2 @ 2 1/2″ × 18″	2 @ 3 1/2″ × 9″
		1 @ 1 1/2″ × 18″	
Each of 3 Lights	1 @ 3 1/2″ × 10 1/2″	1 @ 1 1/2″ × 18″	

Table 9–9. Conversion of Fractional Yards to Inches.

Yards	Inches	Yards	Inches	Yards	Inches
1/8	4 1/2	1 1/8	40 1/2	2 1/8	76 1/2
1/4	9	1 1/4	45	2 1/4	81
3/8	13 1/2	1 3/8	49 1/2	2 3/8	85 1/2
1/2	18	1 1/2	54	2 1/2	90
5/8	22 1/2	1 5/8	58 1/2	2 5/8	94 1/2
3/4	27	1 3/4	63	2 3/4	99
7/8	31 1/2	1 7/8	67 1/2	2 7/8	103 1/2
1	36	2	72	3	108

Table 9–10. Yardage for Ragtime Quilt: 24-Inch Strips of Dark Fabric.

Yardage	Stripping Width	Number of Strips	Strip Length	Inches of Stripping	Number of Pieces of Stripping
4 1/2″	1 1/2″	5	24″	120″	3
4″	2″	2	24″	48″	2
28″	3 1/2″	14	24″	336″	8
Total 36 1/2″					

Yardage for the Pattern Area

The table of strips is the basis for figuring yardage for fabric that will be used in the pattern area. A useful adjunct is Table 9–9, which converts from fractions of a yard to inches.

The easiest quilts to deal with are the ones that require only one or two strips in each fabric. For instance, two strips are needed for most fabrics in the Scrap-bag Come-On Quilt. One strip is 18 and the other 19½ inches long, so their combined length, 37½ inches, is well under the width of the fabric. We need yardage to cover the wider strip, in this case 5½ inches. Referring to Table 9–9, we see that 5½ inches is more than an ⅛ yard, but less than ¼ yard, so we'd buy ¼ yard.

As another example, look at Table 7–4, which shows the strips needed for The Vaults. The strips for this quilt are 76½ inches, which is less than twice the width of fabric, so we need two pieces of stripping for each strip in The Vaults. The strips are 4½ inches wide, so we need 9 inches for each fabric. From Table 9–11, we see that 9 inches is exactly ¼ yard. I'd buy ⅜ yard, because fabric is usually cut off-grain at the store, and because it might fray or shrink when washed.

The situation can become much more complicated when you need many strips of the same fabric. Suppose, for example that you wanted to make the Ragtime quilt, which requires the strips shown in Table 5–7. The strip lengths–19½ inches, 21 inches, and 24 inches—are all less than 45 inches. Two 19½-or 21-inch strips would fit across the width of the fabric pretty easily, but the 24-inch strips present a problem. A 24-inch strip and a 19½-inch strip, which total 43½ inches, might fit across the width of the fabric, but a 24-inch strip and a 21-inch strip, which total 45 inches, probably would not.

I would plan to cut the dark fabric into blocks as shown in Fig. 9–2, including a block a little wider than 19½ inches and a block a little wider than 21 inches. The ten 21-inch strips are all 3½ inches wide, so this block should be a little over 35 inches long. The widths of the 19½-inch strips add up to 35½ inches, so this block should be a little longer. For convenience, I would probably cut both blocks about 36 inches long.

The rest of the fabric will be devoted to cutting stripping for 24-inch strips across the full width of the fabric. I then would cut strips from the stripping, piecing as needed. Table 9–10 shows how to calculate the length of this block. The number of pieces of stripping is obtained by dividing the inches of stripping needed by 45 inches, then rounding up to the nearest whole number. If the number of inches of stripping needed was an exact multiple of 45 inches, I'd round up another number, just because I don't really expect the fabric to be a full 45 inches wide. The total yardage at the bottom of Table 9–10 is a tad over 1 yard; combining this total with the 1 yard need for the top blocks, I'd plan to buy 2⅛ yards of dark fabric.

People often ask for a general rule of thumb for how much fabric to buy; they seem to be hoping for a simple way around calculations like those I've shown here. I suppose I have such a rule of thumb for my own use, since when I'm buying fabric without a particular project in mind I often buy 2 yards. That doesn't mean that 2 yards will be enough for any project; that's just the amount I'm in the habit of buying. That habit is influenced by the fact that I usually use a lot of different fabrics in a quilt, so I often don't need much of any particular fabric. Also, as I mentioned, I've decided that it's okay for me to buy extra fabric.

My frugal side comes to the fore when I'm actually cutting up the fabric. I might have bought extra fabric, but I try to cut out my strips in the most compact, economical way possible. It's often at this point that I go through the process of deciding whether to cut a block of strips, like those for the 19½- and 21-inch strips in the Ragtime quilt, or whether to cut a bunch of stripping and piece out strips, as for the 24-inch strips in Ragtime.

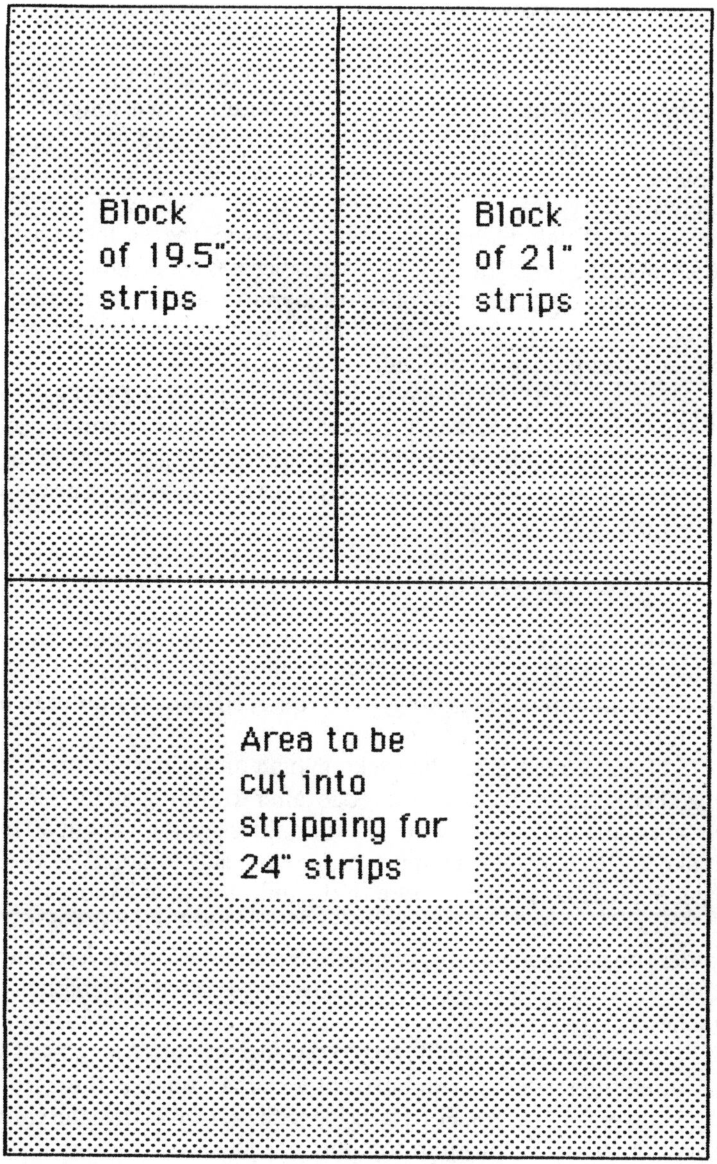

Fig. 9–2. This is a plan for cutting strips for the Ragtime quilt. Blocks of fabric a little over 19½ and 21 inches wide are set aside for the 19½- and 21-inch strips. The 24-inch strips will be cut from stripping cut across the whole width of the fabric in the lower block.

Block of 19.5" strips

Block of 21" strips

Area to be cut into stripping for 24" strips

Yardage for the Borders

Many of the shopping lists for projects in this book list two yardages for borders: one for an unpieced border, and one for a pieced border. The factors that might influence the choice of construction are discussed in Chapter 4. A narrow inner border almost always will be a pieced border, so the yardage needed would be calculated in the same way as the yardage for a wider pieced border.

Border pieces up to 10 or 11 inches wide can be cut from 45-inch wide fabric as shown in Fig. 9–3. Therefore, the yardage needed for an unpieced border is determined by the long border pieces. If the border is mitered, the length of the long border enough excess of some other fabric to cover the binding, you can figure the amount you'll need as follows.

Calculate the area of fabric that you will need for the binding by multiplying the parimeter of the quilt by the width of the binding. For example, a quilt 43 × 55 inches has a perimeter of 110 inches. For 1½-inch-wide binding, I'd need a total area of 165 square inches. How long a piece of 45-inch fabric do you need to get 165 square inches? I'll base my calculations on 40 inches, to allow for shrinkage, selvages, and pieces is the length of the pattern area plus twice the width of the border. If the border is abutted, the length of the long border pieces is usually the length of the pattern area, but occasionally the border piece on the short side of the pattern area actually turns out to be the longer border piece. The length of this border piece is the width of the pattern area plus twice the width of the border.

The yardage for a pieced border is figured like the yardage for stripping used in the pattern area. Calculate the total length of border you'll need, then divide this amount by the width of the fabric and round up to get the number of stripping pieces you'll need. Multiply the number of pieces of stripping by the cut width of the border to get the border yardage.

Yardage for the Backing

The yardage needed for the backing of a quilt depends on whether the backing fabric is wider, by 2 to 4 inches, than the finished quilt top. If the fabric is wide enough to make an unpieced backing, then you need 4 inches more than the length of the quilt top.

If you need to piece the backing, plan on sewing lengths of 45-inch-wide fabric together, selvage edge to selvage edge (after trimming off the selvage) to make a piece of fabric about 85 inches wide. If your quilt is less than about 80 inches long, you can make the backing with a seam running from side to side. The yardage needed for the backing will be twice the width of the quilt top plus 8 inches.

If your quilt is more than about 80 inches long but less than about 80 inches wide, you can make the backing with one seam running vertically in the backing. In this case, the yardage needed for the backing is twice the length of the quilt top, plus 8 inches.

For larger quilts, you'll need to sew together three lengths of fabric. The yardage required for a backing with horizontal seams would be three times the width of the quilt top plus 12 inches. For a backing with vertical seams, the yardage would be three times the length of the quilt top plus 12 inches.

When a quilt is just a little too wide for an unpieced backing, I might not make the usual backing with a horizontal seam since it might be considerably longer than necessary. Suppose, for example, that I had a quilt top that was 50 × 64 inches, so that I needed a backing 54 × 68 inches. This top is too wide for an unpieced backing, but if I sew together two 54-inch lengths of 45-inch-wide fabric, I'll get a backing 54 × about 85 inches and use 3 yards of fabric. I could buy 1¼ times the length of the backing I need (in this case 2⅜ yards of fabric) and cut the extra quarter length into four pieces, which I'd piece to the full length as shown in Fig. 9–3. Many old quilts have backs that look like this example. A back with this kind of extensive

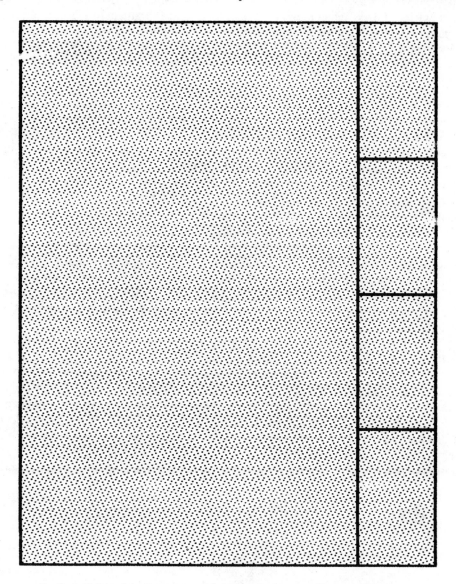

Fig. 9–3. This back has been pieced from the shortest possible yardage of fabric.

piecing makes sense if the backing fabric has a busy pattern that will obscure the seams, if you're really short on fabric, or if you really don't mind seams in the backing.

Yardage for the Binding

Binding requires less fabric than you might think, and often can be cut from excess border or backing fabric, or from excess of one of the fabrics used in the pattern area. If you're buying fabric specifically for binding or want to be sure that you'll have seam allowances and divide 165 by 40, to get 4⅛. In other words, a piece of fabric 40 inches wide and 4⅛ inches long would have an area of 165 square inches. A quarter of a yard (9 inches) of fabric would be plenty. I wouldn't buy less, just because the bias binding pieces would all be very short if they were cut from such a shorter piece of fabric.

ADAPTING DESIGNS

With the nitty-gritty details of bookkeeping and yardage calculation out of the way, we can turn to the fun side of creating new patterns, although even the "fun side" can be intimidating. I think that one of the intimidating things about the idea of creating new patterns is that you only see the completed patterns in a book like this one. You don't see the ones that didn't work out or the messy working drawings with all the corrections in red ink. It might help to know that a designer doesn't go from nothing to a finished pattern in one flash of inspiration.

It also might help to hear that designers don't design "from nothing" in any event. At the very least, they have the memories of all the patterns they've seen and studied tucked away in their unconscious minds. Many, and this certainly includes me, work rather closely from existing patterns. So, suppose you've found a book of patterns. They're all laid out on a grid, and they look like they might be suitable for piecing and repiecing. How do you choose one that really can be adapted, and how do you do it?

The first thing I do when I start poring over a book of designs is to eliminate patterns with X joins, which narrows down the field considerably. It's easy to scan for checkerboard corners, like the joint on the left in Fig. 9–4. More insidious are corners like that on the right in Fig. 9–4, which might not be apparent until the vertical or horizontal lines that represent the seams between segments are drawn in. For example, I am very fond of the key design at the top in Fig. 9–5, but I've never been able to figure out how to piece and repiece it easily. If the design were made of vertical segments there would be eight trouble spots in every repeat of the pattern, while if the design were made with horizontal segments, there would be even more trouble spots.

 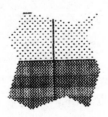

Fig. 9–4. The X-join on the left is easy to spot when you're considering patterns for adaptation to piecing and repiecing. The X-join on the right is not as obvious, but can be just as troublesome.

When I do find a likely looking design in a book I own, I draw in vertical or horizontal seam lines in pencil, directly in the book. With a library book or other borrowed book, draw a copy of the design on graph paper. Next, I check to see what bands the design will require. I put a letter by each segment, identifying the band it would come from. Then I recheck the bands to see whether I can use shifting to reduce the number further.

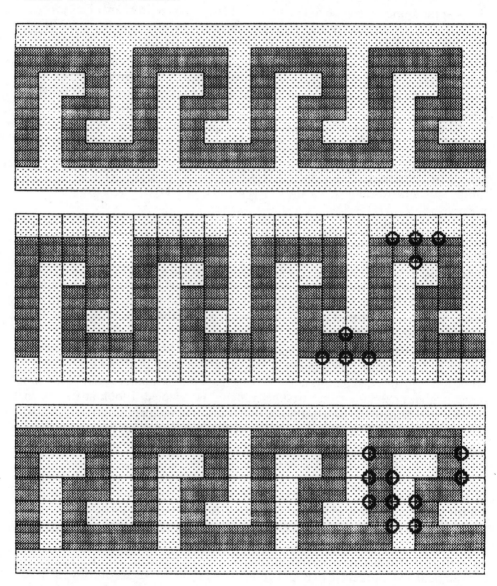

Fig. 9–5. The Greek key pattern at the top is not amenable to piecing and repiecing. If it were pieced of vertical segments, as shown in the middle drawing, the circled X-joins would appear in every repeat of the pattern. Piecing in horizontal segments, as shown in the lower drawing, would produce even more X-joins.

At the same time, I start thinking about how I'll color the design, especially if my design source is in black and white only. The placement of colors in the design might affect the number of bands needed, as we saw with the Hungarian Point patterns. I might do color drawings on graph paper or I might make a line drawing of the pattern, and color photocopies of that. If I want to be completely sure of my choice of fabrics, as when I'm making an especially large or elaborate quilt, I'll actually cut out full-size pieces of the fabrics I propose to use and pin them to a bulletin board. This process uses up a certain amount of fabric, but I can really fine-tune the fabric selection process.

As the design itself is settled, I'll think more about how big I want to make it and how many repeats I'll use. The size might be determined by a bed size, if I'm planning a bed quilt, or it might be determined by the scale of the pattern, the amount of energy I want to put into the project, or other less tangible aethetic considerations.

So finally, I have a finished diagram for the quilt—which may not look terribly finished. I now have a Macintosh computer, with which I can create neat diagrams like those in this book. In the old days, however, I used colored pencil on graph paper, and many of those could be deciphered only by me. Even if your diagram is not a finished artwork, it's enough if it allows you to make up a table of strips, as described previously.

METHODS FOR ORIGINAL DESIGN

We seem to put a premium on originality in design. While in some ways I feel that there's nothing new under the sun, at the same time I feel that my designs, most of which are adapted from other media, are original. Without trying to resolve this paradox, I can offer some techniques for designing other than by starting with someone else's finished design in a book.

One small step is to look for designs outside of books. Somehow a design that you took from a decorative porch railing seems more your own than one taken from a book. I'm so involved in piecing and repiecing that I can't see any vaguely geometric design without checking to see whether it could be adapted. I look at the tile in restrooms, at brickwork, advertising art, upholstery and wallpaper, and the patterns in friends' clothing. When I've been overworking, I see the lines of type in a book as segments in a pieced and repieced quilt. Without going to this extreme, you can keep an eye out for "pieceable" patterns.

Doodling on graph paper is another possibility. This method can be particularly helpful when I've done one quilt, and want to do another one that's a little different. I'll try to find a new way of arranging the motifs, or simpler or more complicated versions of the pattern, or I'll try stretching or compressing parts of the pattern. The pages of sample motifs and zigzag variations in this book are the kind of thing I come up with by doodling.

Sometimes it can help to manipulate things with your hands, too. I'd love to have a big set of square and rectangular blocks or tiles to play with. In the absence of these, I've developed a method for working with paper that I use in my classes. Using a paper cutter, I cut 18-inch strips of various widths from larger size (12-X-18-inch) colored construction paper in lots of different colors.

The designing starts with choosing some colored paper strips, placing them side by side, and "sewing" them together by taping all along the seams with cellophane tape. You'll use a lot of tape, so use a cheap variety. The side with the tape becomes the back side of the band. After you have constructed the paper band, cut it up into segments using a paper cutter, scissors, or rotary cutter.

Constructing the segments was work, but the rest is play. You might make a set of segments with one pattern in mind, and then find that you can use them to make another pattern. You might have made the band with a definite right side up, then find that you can make an interesting pattern by reversing some of the segments. You can play with different arrangements of strips, and with different patterns of shifts. In fact, general undirected play, handling the strips and fooling around with a variety of ideas, can be very productive, as well as being wonderfully relaxing and enjoyable.

These ideas for designing are some that have worked for me. As directions, they're a little vague, partly because, like many designers, I'm not quite sure how I do design. I'm sure there are many other methods, including some that will work particularly well for you. The way to find methods that work is to try them out. Try adapting designs from books and from other media, try distorting or elaborating or otherwise changing a design, and try playing with your design elements. When something works, try it again, and then try variations. Your own methods will emerge. I greatly enjoy designing pieced and repieced quilts; I hope you will, too.

Index

A

abutted corners, 45, 46
acetate, 90
adapting designs, 171
analogous color scheme, 92
Autumn Orchard quilt, 147
   strips for, 147

B

backing, 48
backing yardage
   calculating, 169
bands, 2
bargello, 99
bargello patterns
   Blue Wave, 112
   Gentle Rainbow, 108
   Shazam, 114
   Swags, 116
   The Vaults, 108
basting, 50
batting, 49
binding, 56
binding yardage
   calculating, 171
Blue Wave quilt, 112
   strips for, 113
border yardage
   calculating, 169
borders, 44
Broad-Band Come-On quilt, 34

C

calculating yardage, 165
Center Diamond quilt, 130
   strips for, 131
chaining, 103
changing grid size, 160
changing proportions, 161
   length, 161
   width, 161
Christmas Trees, 80
Christmas Trees runner
   strips for, 83
Christmas Trees tablecloth
   strips for, 83
clarity of color, 92
color, 91
   characteristics of, 91
color arrangements, 93
color schemes, 92
   analogous, 92
   complementary, 92
   monochrome, 92
colors
   choosing, 90

combining fabrics, 95
Come-On place mats, 39
   strips for four, 40
   strips for scrapbag, 41
Come-On quilt
   constructing the quilt, 35
   instructions for, 24
   planning the strips, 25
   strips for broad-band, 34
   strips for scrapbag, 30
   strips for shaded, 32
   strips for two fabrics, 28
complementary color scheme, 92
Corner Diamond quilt, 133
   resizing, 162
   strips for, 134
corner point, 46
corners
   abutted, 45, 46
   mitered, 45, 46
cross-cut lines
   marking, 15
curves
   creating by varying offsets, 108
cutting segments, 22
cutting stripping, 12
cutting tools, 14

D

density of a pattern, 95
design principles, 7
designing quilts, 160
designs, 9
   adapting, 171
   methods for original, 173
Double Peaks place mats, 103
   strips for, 106

E

Eva's Diamonds place mats, 72
   strips for, 71
even-feed foot, 56

F

fabric patterns
   bargello, 108
   Come-On, 24
   half-drop, 122
   multiple-band, 62
   one-band shift, 98
   shifted multiple-band, 122
   two-segment, 62
fabrics
   characteristics of, 90
   choosing, 90
   combining, 95

finished length, 44
Flame Dart quilt, 120
   strips for, 121
florals, 95
foot, 56
frames, 51
full length, 44
Fused Diamonds quilt, 69
   strips for, 69

G

Gentle Rainbow quilt, 108
   resizing, 162
   strips for, 109
geometrics, 95
gradations of color, 93
grid size
   changing, 160

H

half-drop patterns, 122, 127
   Autumn Orchard, 147
   Center Diamond, 130
   Corner Diamond, 133
   Heart Throb, 134
   Orchard, 143
   Peacock Eyes, 139
   Spring Tender, 149
hand quilting, 52
   equipment for, 51
Heart Throb quilt, 134
   patterns for, 138
   strips for, 135
hoops, 51
hue, 91
Hungarian Point, 153
Hungarian Point patterns
   Hungarian Spires, 158
   Standing Wave, 155
Hungarian Spires quilt, 158
   strips for, 159

K

kite, 149

L

length
   changing, 161
   finished, 44
   full, 44
loop-and-shift technique, 99
   directions for, 103
lozenge, 149

M

making a paper template, 16
marking cross-cut lines, 15
marking stripping, 15
marking the quilting pattern, 49
marking tools, 14
matching, 21
mitered corners, 45, 46
monochrome color scheme, 92
multiple-band patterns

Christmas Trees, 80
   other, 74
   Ragtime, 80
   three-band, 67
   two-segment, 62

N

near-solids, 96
new pattern
   preparing a table for, 163

O

one-band shift patterns, 98
   Blue Wave, 112
   Double Peaks, 103
   Flame Dart, 120
   Gentle Rainbow, 108
   other variations, 112
   Shazam, 114
   Swags, 116
   The Vaults, 108
   Zigzag, 99
Orchard quilt, 143
   strips for, 143
original design
   methods for, 173

P

pattern, 2
   density of, 95
   marking the quilting, 49
   scale of, 94
   structures of, 95
   table for a new, 163
pattern area
   yardage for, 167
pattern structures
   florals, 95
   geometrics, 95
   near-solids, 96
   prints, 95
   stripey prints, 95
patterns
   bargello, 108
   Come-On, 24
   half-drop, 122
   Hungarian Point, 153
   multiple-band, 62
   one-band shift, 98
   shifted multiple-band, 122
   two-segment, 62
Peacock Eyes quilt, 139
piecing
   strip, 7
piecing within strips, 20
pillow method, 39
pinning, 21
place mats
   Come-On, 39
   Double Peaks, 106
   Eva's Diamonds, 71
Plus Signs quilt, 122

strips for, 123
principles
    design, 7
prints, 95
    stripey, 95
proportions
    changing, 161

Q

quilting, 2, 44, 50
    hand, 52
    strip, 7
quilting in the ditch, 37
quilting pattern
    marking the, 49
quilting thread, 52
quilts
    designing your own, 160
    resizing, 160
    signing the, 60

R

Ragtime quilt, 80
    strips for, 86
    strips for dark fabric, 166
resizing quilts, 160
roller foot, 56
row, 99
running stitches, 53

S

scale of a pattern, 94
Scrapbag Come-On quilt, 30
segments, 2
    cutting and sewing, 22
sewing machine, 21
sewing machine foot
    even-feed, 56
    roller, 56
    straight-stitch presser, 56
sewing segments, 22
sewing strips together, 20
Shaded Come-On quilt, 32
Shazam quilt, 114
    strips for, 114
shifted multiple-band patterns
    Plus Signs, 122
    Ziggurats, 126
signing the quilt, 60
Spring Tender quilt, 149
    strips for, 150
Standing Wave quilt, 155
    strips for, 155
stitches
    running, 53
straight-stitch presser foot, 56
strip piecing, 7
strip quilting, 7
Striped Sampler quilt, 74
    resizing, 162
    strips for, 76
stripey prints, 95

stripping, 13
    cutting, 12
    marking, 15
strips, 2
    piecing within, 20
    sewing together, 20
structures of a pattern, 95
Summer/Winter Weave quilt, 62
    strips for, 64
Swags album cover
    strips for, 118
Swags quilt, 116

T

T-joins, 7
table
    preparing for a new pattern, 163
template
    making a, 16
    using the, 16
The Vaults quilt, 108
    strips for, 112
thread
    quilting, 52
three-band patterns
    Eva's Diamonds, 72
    Fused Diamonds, 67
    Striped Sampler, 74
tools
    cutting, 14
    marking, 14
tools for hand quilting, 51
two-segment patterns
    Summer/Winter Weave, 62

U

using the paper template, 16

V

value, 91
varying offsets
    use in creating curves, 108

W

width
    changing, 161
window, 94

X

X-joins, 7

Y

yardage
    calculating backing, 169
    calculating binding, 171
    calculating pattern, 167
    calculating border, 169
    figuring, 165

Z

Ziggurats quilt, 126
    strips for, 126
Zigzag quilt, 99
    strips for, 99